At his best, man is the noblest of all animals; separated from law and justice he is the worst.

Aristotle

If we're destroying our trees and destroying our environment and hurting animals and hurting one another and all that stuff, there's got to be a very powerful energy to fight that. I think we need more love in the world. We need more kindness, more compassion, more joy, more laughter. I definitely want to contribute to that.

Ellen DeGeneres

Humans aren't as good as we should be in our capacity to empathize with feelings and thoughts of others, be they humans or other animals on Earth. So maybe part of our formal education should be training in empathy. Imagine how different the world would be if, in fact, that were 'reading, writing, arithmetic, empathy.'

Neil deGrasse Tyson

Cats are very independent animals. They're very sexy, if you want. Dogs are different. They're familiar. They're obedient. You call a cat, you go, 'Cat, come here.' He doesn't come to you unless you have something in your hand that he thinks might be food. They're very free animals, and I like that.

Antonio Banderas

The greatness of a nation can be judged by the way its animals are treated.

Mahatma Gandhi

If having a soul means being able to feel love and loyalty and gratitude, then animals are better off than a lot of humans.

James Herriot

Animals are such agreeable friends - they ask no questions; they pass no criticisms.

George Eliot

He who is cruel to animals becomes hard also in his dealings with men. We can judge the heart of a man by his treatment of animals.

Immanuel Kant

Animals have come to mean so much in our lives. We live in a fragmented and disconnected culture. Politics are ugly, religion is struggling, technology is stressful, and the economy is unfortunate. What's one thing that we have in our lives that we can depend on? A dog or a cat loving us unconditionally, every day, very faithfully.

Jon Katz

As a spiritual person, nature for me has always been a healing place. Going back all the way to my childhood on the farm, the fields and forests were places of adventure and self-discovery. Animals were companions and friends, and the world moved at a slower, more rational pace than the bustling cities where I'd resided my adult life.

David Mixner

We have two dogs, Mabel and Wolf, and three cats at home, Charlie, George and Chairman. We have two cats on our farm, Tom and Little Sister, two horses, and two mini horses, Hannah and Tricky. We also have two cows, Holy and Madonna. And those are only the animals we let sleep in our bed.

Ellen DeGeneres

A man can live and be healthy without killing animals for food; therefore, if he eats meat, he participates in taking animal life merely for the sake of his appetite.

Leo Tolstoy

Animals are reliable, many full of love, true in their affections, predictable in their actions, grateful and loyal. Difficult standards for people to live up to.

Alfred A. Montapert

I'm lucky because I have a job I love. I really miss being away from home, being in my own bed, seeing my animals and siblings, having my moms cookies. I have a couple cats. I got a kitten about a year ago and now Im going on the road so I wont see him for a while. I feel bad.

Michelle Branch

People who have no hold over their process of thinking are likely to be ruined by liberty of thought. If thought is immature, liberty of thought becomes a method of converting men into animals.

Muhammad Iqbal

These are the animals that are the reason why you don't see old animals in the wild. You don't see sick animals in the wild. You don't see lame animals in the wild, and its all because of the predator: the lion, the tiger, the leopard, all the cats.

Tippi Hedren

One who is kind is sympathetic and gentle with others. He is considerate of others' feelings and courteous in his behavior. He has a helpful nature. Kindness pardons others' weaknesses and faults. Kindness is extended to all - to the aged and the young, to animals, to those low of station as well as the high.

Ezra Taft Benson

I can find God in nature, in animals, in birds and the environment.

Pat Buckley

All animals are equal, but some animals are more equal than others.

George Orwell

I'm concentrating on staying healthy, having peace, being happy, remembering what is important, taking in nature and animals, spending time reading, trying to understand the universe, where science and the spiritual meet.

Joan Jett

When I was younger, my family would go camping and fishing on our ranches. My dad loves being around all kinds of animals. He's the one who got me to be a really big animal lover.

Paris Hilton

If anyone has seen the horrific and unwatchable footage of the Chinese cat and dog trade - animals skinned alive - then they could not possibly argue in favour of China as a caring nation. There are no animal protection laws in China and this results in the worst animal abuse and cruelty on the planet. It is indefensible.

Steven Patrick Morrissey

Animals, whom we have made our slaves, we do not like to consider our equal.

Charles Darwin

I like some animals more than some people, some people more than some animals.

Jane Goodall

You look at a herd of cattle and well, they all look the same... but they know. They all have an individual personality, and those personalities change from day to day. They can have their grumpy days and their happy days and their serene days. But it's unpredictable. You can't be off in outer space when you're dealing with animals.

Chris Cooper

As a child. I grew up on a small farm, so I did a lot of drawings of animals, chickens and people. At the bottom of every page, I'd put a strange scribble. I was emulating adult handwriting, though I didn't actually know how to write.

Joyce Carol Oates

The intuitive connection children feel with animals can be a tremendous source of joy. The unconditional love received from pets, and the lack of artifice in the relationship, contrast sharply with the much trickier dealings with members of their own species.

Frans de Waal

I love things made out of animals. It's just so funny to think of someone saying, 'I need a letter opener. I guess I'll have to kill a deer.

David Sedaris

Man can acquire accomplishments or he can become an animal, whichever he wants. God makes the animals, man makes himself.

Alfred North Whitehead

What's cool is when you're able to give your audience imagination and you don't have to cage them in like animals.

Shia LaBeouf

Animals are near and dear to my heart, and I've devoted my life to trying to improve their lives.

Betty White

I know at last what distinguishes man from animals; financial worries.

Romain Rolland

I'm very involved with PETA - People for Ethical Treatment of Animals - and Greenpeace and a lot of women's shelter and clothing giveaways.

Pink

My mother said that we're so lucky to be women. It's not that men are weak. Men are men. We're two completely different animals.

Diane von Furstenberg

I don't think we're going to save anything if we go around talking about saving plants and animals only; we've got to translate that into what's in it for us.

Jim Fowler

I'd say the best is when I was in Africa, I saw a hippo in a house. Someone had a pet hippo. And they're meant to be one of the most dangerous animals on the planet, and they had one that was sort of just wandering in and out of their house, just sort of roaming about.

Karl Pilkington

There have only been about a half dozen genuinely important events in the four-billion-year saga of life on Earth: single-celled life, multicelled life, differentiation into plants and animals, movement of animals from water to land, and the advent of mammals and consciousness.

Elon Musk

I needed a place to put the dogs. The prisoners ruined the jail, so I put the prisoners in the tents and I had a nice place to put the dogs. We treat the cats nice too, and horses. I have the inmates take care of the animals. It's therapy too, you see.

Joe Arpaio

Attempts to defend amusement parks and circuses on the grounds that they 'educate' people about animals should not be taken seriously. Such enterprises are part of the commercial entertainment industry. The most important lesson they teach impressionable young minds is that it is acceptable to keep animals in captivity for human amusement.

Peter Singer

If you watch animals objectively for any length of time, you're driven to the conclusion that their main aim in life is to pass on their genes to the next generation.

David Attenborough

I'm a radical environmentalist; I think the sooner we asphyxiate in our own filth, the better. The world will do better without us. Maybe some fuzzy animals will go with us, but there'll be plenty of other animals, and they'll be back.

Anthony Bourdain

It is hard to get animals which normally pay little attention to each other to do things together. One can teach dolphins to jump simultaneously out of the water precisely because they show similar behavior spontaneously, but try to make two domestic cats jump together and you will fail.

Frans de Waal

When I was a kid, I used to imagine animals running under my bed. I told my dad, and he solved the problem quickly.

He cut the legs off the bed.

Lou Brock

When fish experience something that would cause other animals physical pain, they behave in ways suggestive of pain, and the change in behaviour may last several hours.

Peter Singer

As social animals, we need to exchange juicy tales about someone - to connect with one another. For millions of years our forebears must have sat around the campfire, whispering about everyone they knew.

Helen Fisher

Animals come from nature. They were not designed. All my inspiration comes from nature, whether it's an animal or the layout of bark or of a leaf. Sometimes my patterns are very bold, and you can barely see where they come from, but all the textures and all the prints come out of nature.

Diane von Furstenberg

Among irrational animals the love of the offspring and of

the parents for each other is extraordinary because God, who created them, compensated for the deficiency of reason by the superiority of their senses.

Saint Basil

Several countries - among them Austria, Costa Rica, Denmark, Finland, India, Israel and Sweden - ban or severely restrict the use of wild animals in circuses. In Brazil, a movement to ban wild animals from circuses started after hungry lions managed to grab and devour a small boy.

Peter Singer

There is no kind way to rip the skin off animals' backs. Anyone who wears any fur shares the blame for the torture and gruesome deaths of millions of animals each year.

Natalie Imbruglia

Animals don't have anyone to protect them. If we don't stand up, the people who are harming animals will never get stopped.

Paul Rodriguez

We ended up moving out to Texas. We live outside of Austin. We've got a couple horses, we've got three miniature donkeys, we've got four dogs. Miniature donkeys are very warm, loving animals.

Kyle Chandler

People on death row, the treatment of animals, women's right to choose. So much in America is based on religious fundamentalist Christianity. Grow up! This is the modern world!

Eddie Vedder

I collect stuffed animals, and toy stores make me happy.

Grace Slick

There is an overabundance of rational reasons to say no to factory-farmed meat: It is the No. 1 cause of global warming, it systematically forces tens of billions of animals to suffer in ways that would be illegal if they were dogs, it is a decisive factor in the development of swine and avian flus, and so on.

Jonathan Safran Foer

I don't look like a desert person because I stay indoors most of the day and fool around at night. That's what the desert animals do - they don't have a tan either.

Don Van Vliet

I was very independent growing up, but there were things that were bothering me that I never told anybody. I would talk to our animals at home.

Janet Jackson

In most countries, it is possible to visit zoos and see bored animals pacing back and forth in cages, with nothing to do but wait for the next meal. Circuses are even worse places for animals. Their living conditions are deplorable, especially in travelling circuses where cages have to be small so that they can go on the road.

Peter Singer

So, basically, my view is I don't want to support the exploitation of animals, and within reason, I will do what I can to avoid it, but it's not like it's a religion for me. It's not like I consider I'm polluted if somehow some bit of milk or cheese or something passes my lips.

Peter Singer

I became a vegetarian out of compassion for animals and to live as healthy as possible. I realized soon after that I was truly concerned with nonviolent consumption and my own health, a vegan diet was the best decision.

Davey Havok

I am interested in a lot of things - not just show business and my passion for animals. I try to keep current in what's going on in the world. I do mental exercises. I don't have any trouble memorizing lines because of the crossword puzzles I do every day to keep my mind a little limber. I don't sit and vegetate.

Betty White

The health of the planet is at stake, because the cruelty and the waste that accompanies the slaughter of billions of animals each year literally infects us all. We could consume healthy plant-based food produced at almost infinitely less cost. What does that say, really, about us and what we're doing... to animals and to ourselves?

James Cromwell

A growing and increasingly influential movement of

philosophers, ethicists, law professors and activists are convinced that the great moral struggle of our time will be for the rights of animals.

Michael Pollan

For at the same time many people seem eager to extend the circle of our moral consideration to animals, in our factory farms and laboratories we are inflicting more suffering on more animals than at any time in history.

Michael Pollan

Man has done a lot to make himself dangerous and animals get the worst of all of it. But then, man too is an animal.

Don Van Vliet

I have held healthy respects of bears along with assorted crocodiles, snakes and lots of other animals. You know, bears are dangerous, you have to be super careful.

Bear Grylls

There was such a relationship between the buffalo and the American Indian - the Indians would eat them, live inside their pelts, use every part of the body. There was almost no separation between the people and the animals.

Val Kilmer

I got my love of animals from the Dr. Doolittle books and my love of Africa from the Tarzan novels. I remember my mum taking me to the first Tarzan film, which starred Johnny Weissmuller, and bursting into tears. It wasn't what I had imagined at all.

Jane Goodall

Animals keep you company when you're really lonely. It helps because when you have a friend around who always likes you no matter what - it's harder to feel bad or down.

Aaron Carter

I grew up in a home where animals were ever-present and often dominated our lives. There were always horses, dogs, and cats, as well as a revolving infirmary of injured wildlife being nursed by my sister the aspiring vet.

Julia Glass

I feel as if I go to Africa, I may never come back. I'm just going to live with the animals and adopt an elephant, and it's going to be my friend.

Dianna Agron

Being able and willing to complain is what makes us rational and moral animals, capable of seeing and articulating the difference between how things are and how they should be.

Julian Baggini

I think growing up on a farm in a certain amount of isolation, with not a lot of friends nearby, makes you entertain yourself and kind of grows your imagination - being alone is quite good for all that. You make up stories, talk to the animals, let them be an audience, a bunch of cows.

Kristen Schaal

I dressed up as a veterinarian for a Halloween costume party. I had the lab coat. I got a couple of stuffed animals for patients and put bandages on them.

Tracy Chapman

Before I became famous I had a very full life, and that gave me a lot to pick from. I always use everything. It always comes in handy. Working with animals... Well, I just enjoyed that. That was the most peaceful time.

Cyndi Lauper

Though not a natural world by any means, more like a collection of living dioramas, a zoo exists in its own time zone, somewhere between the seasonal sense of animals and our madly ticking watch time.

Diane Ackerman

We see the moon, don't we? So it's our eye. Animals see us, don't they? So we're their animals.

Don Van Vliet

Unlike the primate hand, the elephant's grasping organ is also its nose. Elephants use their trunks not only to reach food but also to sniff and touch it. With their unparalleled sense of smell, the animals know exactly what they are going for. Vision is secondary.

Frans de Waal

The undisturbed coastal plain is home to a wide variety of plants and animals and is the only wilderness sanctuary in North America that protects a complete range of the arctic ecosystem.

Dan Lipinski

Federal legislation is urgently needed to stop this insanity of wild animals in captivity.

Tippi Hedren

Animals awaken, first facially, then bodily. Men's bodies wake before their faces do. The animal sleeps within its body, man sleeps with his body in his mind.

Malcolm de Chazal

If anything, the bailouts actually hindered lending, as banks became more like house pets that grow fat and lazy on two guaranteed meals a day than wild animals that have to go out into the jungle and hunt for opportunities in order to eat.

Matt Taibbi

I've had a love of animals from birth. I love getting to know other species. We should all be aware that there is not one thing we can give a wild animal in captivity that they need.

Tippi Hedren

Farming with live animals is a 7 day a week, legal form of slavery.

George Segal

The most important thing is to preserve the world we live in. Unless people understand and learn about our world, habitats, and animals, they won't understand that if we don't protect those habitats, we'll eventually destroy ourselves.

Jack Hanna

I try to keep a positive intention and use whatever resources I have to benefit others. I try to create businesses that I think are not hurtful. I try to do things that I think are helpful to the environment, to the animals, and to the planet.

Russell Simmons

We ogle plants and animals up close on television, the Internet and in the movies. We may not worship the animals we see, but we still regard them as necessary physical and spiritual companions. Technological nature can't completely satisfy that yearning.

Diane Ackerman

When we seed millions of acres of land with these plants, what happens to foraging birds, to insects, to microbes, to the other animals, when they come in contact and digest plants that are producing materials ranging from plastics to vaccines to pharmaceutical products?

Jeremy Rifkin

Bolivia's majority Indian population was always excluded, politically oppressed and culturally alienated. Our national wealth, our raw materials, was plundered. Indios were once treated like animals here. In the 1930s and 40s, they were sprayed with DDT to kill the vermin on their skin and in their hair whenever they came into the city.

Evo Morales

Genesis 9 is where the animals went wild, and God gave

them wildness. After the flood, that's when he made animals wild. Up until that time, everybody was vegetarian.

Phil Robertson

I've always loved animals and I always thought that they were, if not better, then the absolute equal of any two legged creature that God ever created.

Ali MacGraw

I've always had a repulsion going in a place where animals are in captivity.

Marion Cotillard

I think if you're against cruelty and you look at what happens to animals in slaughterhouses and on factory farms, you have to be completely against eating meat.

Ingrid Newkirk

If people could be as honest as animals, what a different world it would be.

Tippi Hedren

I've just always loved animals.

Doris Day

When my parents went off to Knoxville to work, I lived with my father's mother. She was strict - the kind who starched and ironed dresses. I had to sit more than I played. Oh, I was miserable. I liked being out with the animals. I'd come in the house with my hair pulled out, sash off the dress, dirty as heck. I was always getting spanked.

Tina Turner

I never thought I could learn much from a dog or cat. They sleep when we sleep. They eat when we eat. I'm into observing animals being as wild as they can be in a captive environment.

Dominic Monaghan

It goes without saying that the desire to accomplish the task with more confidence, to avoid wasting time and labour, and to spare our experimental animals as much as possible, made us strictly observe all the precautions taken by surgeons in respect to their patients.

Ivan Pavlov

PETA has a proven track record of success. Each victory
PETA wins for the animals is a stepping stone upon which
we build a more compassionate world for all beings - and
we will never give up our fight until all animals are treated
with respect and kindness.

Bea Arthur

I have such a passion because I adore animals so much.

Lea Michele

My guiltiest pleasure? 'Untamed & Uncut'. Videos of
people being attacked by animals. Yeah. I don't know why.
I just love seeing guys who say, 'I'm gonna stick my hand
in that crocodile's mouth and see what happens.' And then it
snaps down on them. There you go - that's what you get!
It's a wild animal, my friend.

Nathan Fillion

I'm definitely an animal lover, and I stand up for all
animals' rights.

Laura Mennell

A good breeder or experienced rescue agency wants you to prove that you'll be a capable caretaker. The interrogation and screening can be annoying, but it's also a sign that you're on the right track. A breeder ought to know if you work long hours away from home, have a fenced yard, have kids or other animals, or if you have access to parks.

Jon Katz

Lots of people talk to animals... Not very many listen, though... That's the problem.

Benjamin Hoff

Your body's made to run, to walk, to trek long distances and carry things, work in a forest, and hunt animals. You have to keep it alive to function.

Dolph Lundgren

Drinking when we are not thirsty and making love at all seasons, madam: that is all there is to distinguish us from other animals.

Pierre Beaumarchais

Well I do find the beauty in animals. I find beauty everywhere. I find beauty in my garden.

Doris Day

I get along very well with animals and children. I dig them, I get them.

Zoe Saldana

I find solace in animals. I have got a stray dog at home called Candy. I picked it up while I was waiting at the airport one day. I always wanted to have a 'macho' dog but got this sweet little thing instead.

Randeep Hooda

I used to help my grandfather on the farm, driving tractors, raising crops and animals. I used to feed some of the baby cows and pigs, and I had to be no older than 7 or 8. Then at about 9 or 10 I started driving tractors. It showed me at an early age what hard work was all about and how dedicated you have to be, no matter what you do.

Tyson Chandler

I'm not perfect and I know it. I've done all sorts of things that are frowned upon these days - big-game hunting, fishing. I still enjoy fishing but I don't kill warm-blooded animals any more - I make an exception with birds sometimes.

Wilbur Smith

Even if people do wrong, we're social animals, so what can we do about stopping them doing the same things in future? Saying people are 'bad' or 'evil' is just an unwillingness to engage; an unwillingness to try to empathise. That sanctimonious attitude doesn't help anyone.

Denise Mina

I want to be an entrepreneur too; I like the business side of things. When I was younger I wanted to be a vet or a tightrope walker. But I have no sense of balance and I can't bear animals dying, so I abandoned both ideas.

Georgia Jagger

Human's can't live in the present as animals do; they just

live in the present. But human's are always thinking about the future or the past.

Townes Van Zandt

If you look at little kids and wild animals, these are two groups of things that whenever I'm with them forces me to be in the moment.

Dominic Monaghan

In my movies, there has been little to do in the way of animal rights. I have never worked in a movie with animals. No horse-riding, no trained dogs, lions, bears. A few actors, but what could I do? We had to have them.

Casey Affleck

The main point for me is moral; animals are sentient beings. I know for some this is a hard argument to accept, but we're not built to eat a lot of meat.

Grace Slick

As long as man eats animals how can cruelty to animals be removed.

Morarji Desai

The important thing is that we now have the tools to sequence all kinds of animals and plants and microbes - as well as humans. It is not important that we didn't actually finish the human sequence yet.

Freeman Dyson

Turns out, I couldn't catch them - or even get close to them. I realized that sharks are amazing, beautiful animals who have absolutely no interest in checking me out.

Malin Akerman

It isn't true that convicts live like animals: animals have more room to move around.

Mario Vargas Llosa

Since we can't count on the meat, egg, and dairy industries to protect animals from the most egregious forms of cruelty, what can we, as consumers, do? Opting out of paying someone to allow animals to die in a barn fire or at the slaughterhouse seems pretty reasonable.

Ingrid Newkirk

When you're dealing with a problem as complex as autism, you have to look at it from many different points of view and assemble evidence from many different vantage points. Biological evidence in humans and in animals, toxicologic evidence, how does the body deal with toxins, and evidence looking at the actual experience in populations.

Harvey V. Fineberg

Closeness to animals creates the desire to understand them, and not just a little piece of them, but the whole animal. It makes us wonder what goes on in their heads even though we fully realize that the answer can only be approximated.

Frans de Waal

Scientists are supposed to study animals in a totally objective fashion, similar to the way we inspect a rock or measure the circumference of a tree trunk. Emotions are not to interfere with the assessment. The animal-rights movement capitalizes on this perception, depicting scientists as devoid of compassion.

Frans de Waal

I love animals and I love to see movies with animals that are done respectfully, you know?

Kristin Davis

It more or less has the shape of a love song, but 'Crescent Moon' reflects more my longing for an ancient romantic context that includes wild animals, fire, danger of death, stellar navigation, and seasonal intuition.

Frank Black

I love animals, and I feel more of a connection to animals than people.

Kaley Cuoco

Unlike New Zealand, which has nothing especially predatory, Australia is full of spiders and crocodiles and all kinds of animals that will eat you and sting you.

Brian Cox

Sharks are really serious animals. They've been around longer than dinosaurs. They're basically prehistoric killing machines, and that's terrifying and fascinating, at the same time.

Sara Paxton

Doctors are human animals. They want to be loved, they are tribal, they instinctually favor stories over scientific evidence, they make mistakes, and even small gifts make them susceptible to being biased.

Alice Dreger

If you put a real leaf and a silk leaf side by side, you'll see something of the difference between Homer's poetry and anyone else's. There seem to be real leaves still alive in the 'Iliad,' real animals, real people, real light attending everything.

Alice Oswald

Abuse yourself all you want - just leave animals out of it. Don't wear fur.

Steve-O

We, as a people, we have a strong need to categorize everything. We put labels on everything and it's a totally understandable need because we are animals and we need to understand order and where to fit in.

Armin van Buuren

Like the herd animals we are, we sniff warily at the strange one among us.

Loren Eiseley

Certainly it is wrong to be cruel to animals and the destruction of a whole species can be a great evil. The capacity for feelings of pleasure and pain and for the form of life of which animals are capable clearly impose duties of compassion and humanity in their case.

John Rawls

Working with animals is always going to be tough because the animal doesn't know it's an actor.

Kit Harington

I just think you would never kill and cut up a human to wear so why do it to animals? I just think it's horrible, I would never wear fur, although I guess if it was a really vintage piece you might just get away with it.

Kelly Osbourne

I am not brutal or cruel to animals. My mission has always been to save dogs - especially troubled and abandoned dogs. I've dedicated my life to this.

Cesar Millan

Some rescue groups are highly organized, experienced, well-funded, nearly professional. Others are small amateur operations run out of garages and back yards. Their members may identify strongly with animals as victims, sometimes because of traumas and disappointments in their own lives. Others simply love animals and want to help them.

Jon Katz

Most modern Indians don't stick to their caste jobs any more. There is more inter-caste marriage, more fluidity, more freedom than ever before. But the outcastes are usually still outcastes, because they are still the ones who tan India's animals, burn its dead, and remove its excrement.

Rose George

I think that animals aren't less intelligent than humans, they're just of a different intelligence. We have five million smell-sensitive cells in our nose, they have two hundred and fifty million - they can smell emotion. They can smell different types of emotion, they just have another type of intelligence.

Mike Mills

'Meat' is a vague term and can be used to refer to many parts of an animal, including internal organs and skin. For the most part, the meat we eat consists of muscle tissue taken from farm animals, whether it's a sirloin steak, which is cut from the rear of a cow, or a pork chop, taken from flesh near the spine of a pig.

Michael Specter

Animals in general have always been my passion, project, crusade - whatever you want to call it! The ocean is such a huge, beautiful thing that I feel like we all take for granted.

Aimee Teegarden

I love them very much. All animals big and small. You can name an ant for instance.

Bindi Irwin

The case for exploiting animals for food, clothing and entertainment often relies on our superior intelligence, language and self-awareness: the rights of the superior being trump those of the inferior.

Michael Shermer

I don't need that much to live - we don't need that much to have a wonderful life. I learned that from animals.

Carrie Ann Inaba

My dad, Donald, was a vet and had a practice in Yorkshire. Cats and dogs were his bread and butter, but his greatest love was large animals.

Alastair Campbell

All of my friends are animal people. To me, cats are people, too. Animals are people, too. I travel a lot and when I go overseas, it's really hard on me because the animals are treated much differently, especially in developing countries.

AnnaLynne McCord

I don't eat animals. I rescue strays and take injured pigeons to the wildlife rehab. I carry spiders and wasps outside in a cup covered with a 3x5 card. It would only follow that I'd take pause when contemplating the abrupt and apparently brutal ending of a tiny human being's life, or even a potential human being's life.

Victoria Moran

I'm interested in raw land and trees and fresh air and rivers and lots of animals around them.

Kent McCord

When I was younger, I wanted to be a vet or a tightrope walker. But I have no sense of balance, and I can't bear animals dying, so I abandoned both ideas.

Georgia May Jagger

Well, I had an immense respect for Cirque du Soleil when I first say them in the '80s on a television show and just thought, you know, this group is really reinventing the circus, as you know. Because there wasn't three rings.

There were no animals.

Criss Angel

There is a descent from God through the world to animals, and an ascent from animals through the world to God. He is the highest point of the scale, pure act and active power, the purest light.

Giordano Bruno

There are so many ingredients that are contained in 'The Wall' that were not necessarily contained in other Pink Floyd records, particularly following on from 'Animals,' which was very spare and sparse. Production on it was much more massive, the complexity of the recording was much more intense.

Nick Mason

I was a town child, it is true, but that did not prevent me enjoying open-air life, with plants and animals.

Georg Brandes

I have a tough stomach, and I've put myself through a lot.

But when I first found out what happens to animals on modern factory farms and in today's slaughterhouses, I wanted to throw up - I literally couldn't believe it.

Steve-O

The Indians could not undertake any widespread cultivation of the plains not only because they lacked iron tools but also because they had no draft animals.

Ellsworth Huntington

Starvation and disease are the original weapons of mass destruction. When you burn fields and kill animals, people are left vulnerable.

James Nachtwey

Learning about factory farms and their horrendous treatment of animals is what made me become vegetarian in the first place. I also support the education of the public on adopting pets from animal shelters or saving homeless animals off the street in lieu of buying them from pet shops.

Laura Mennell

Some of the best things about being a vegetarian include, of course, contributing towards the welfare of animals. Being a vegetarian can also make you a healthier person, and it helps the environment. All of these things make vegetarianism worthwhile. It's really a win-win situation.

Laura Mennell

I'm killing two birds at once, so to speak. Animal-based food kills people. This way, by going vegan... we get healthy and save animals. I'm being selfish, too, because if I can get my employees healthier, we cut down on sick days and gain more productivity.

Steve Wynn

Strictly speaking, my interest is not in legal rights for animals but in a change of heart towards animals.

J. M. Coetzee

The most important of all rights is the right to life, and I cannot foresee a day when domesticated animals will be granted that right in law.

J. M. Coetzee

All of us from fertile egg to embryo to corpse, are exactly that: warm, wet, furry animals compelled by the sexuality of our forefathers and foremothers to be, either directly or indirectly, our own exciting and excitable, provocative and provocable selves.

Lynn Margulis

From the physical point of view, a man is nothing more than a system of cells, or from the mental point of view, than a system of representations; in either case, he differs only in degree from animals.

Emile Durkheim

I'm such a weirdo. I'm animal-mad, so my ideal date would probably be something involving going to see animals.

Sheridan Smith

Predators make it much more difficult to find consensus. It's a lot easier to agree about birds and plants than about animals that endanger people and livestock.

Gale Norton

I have always loved animals, and as a child, I read a lot of horse books. I had a particular favorite called 'Silver Snaffles' that my mother gave away.

Drew Gilpin Faust

As far as the Animals breaking up - it was my fault. I wanted out. We took it to the max, as far as we could take it. Our reunion tour in 1983 went pretty good until we left America. Then we pushed it too hard and it fell apart.

Eric Burdon

I look upon The Animals, they were a great band initially, we left our mark, but thing was it was a band that couldn't live up to its name so I soldiered on. On one level, it was devastating for a while. On another level, maybe I should thank them for helping me make my own way in my own career.

Eric Burdon

Pandemics do not occur randomly. From malaria and influenza to AIDS and SARS, the lethal microbes have come, in the first instance, from animals, especially wild animals. And we increasingly know which parts of the world pose the greatest risk for future incursions.

Nathan Wolfe

Humans like to think of themselves as unusual. We've got big brains that make it possible for us to think, and we think that we have free will and that our behavior can't be described by some mechanistic set of theorems or ideas. But even in terms of much of our behavior, we really aren't very different from other animals.

Mark Pagel

There are good intentions behind many people's conversion to veganism, including an admirable devotion to the well-being of animals and a justified skepticism about the crap the USDA allows manufacturers to put in our food. But it's hard to ignore the often sanctimonious nature of what some nutritionists view as an 'extremist' way of eating.

Julie Klausner

I grew up on a farm and my grandfather quit school when he was 12, but when it came to common sense and animals, he was the smartest person I've ever met, before or since. He taught me that to touch an animal is an earned privilege. It's not a right.

Ian Dunbar

Werewolves are much more common animals than you might think.

Daniel Pinkwater

Wild animals are just as confused as people are now. You've got toxins in the water, oil, sewage, all sorts of things.

Jack Hannah

You can tell all you need to about a society from how it treats animals and beaches.

Frank Deford

It's not hard to draw from within yourself to play someone protective of her daughter. I have animals and I'm a daughter, sister, wife, aunt and friend, and I can be fiercely protective.

Tricia Helfer

Although I agree that wild horses are a symbol of the American West, I also believe that it is the responsibility of

Congress to ensure that these animals are managed, protected, and controlled in an effective manner.

Jon Porter

I've done everything from cater, wait tables, pre-school teacher, painting, to being Cinderella, Elmo, a clown, nanny, selling hair... I would do kid's parties and entertain and do magic and paint faces and balloon animals. The highlight of my life.

Diora Baird

I had a ton of animals; I had a goat growing up, a bunch of rabbits, a vegetable garden.

Kelli Williams

Heartless though it may seem to some, among the least harmful things to eat are sustainably culled wild animals. In the absence of natural predators, deer populations in parts of Britain have reached such dense numbers that the woodlands they browse fail to regenerate.

Tristram Stuart

It's fair to say when you go out and walk in the woods or on a beach, the most conspicuous forms of life you will see are plants and animals, and certainly there's a huge diversity of those types of organisms, perhaps 10 million animal species and several hundred thousand plant species.

Andrew H. Knoll

Many years ago it was taught that plants and animals were composed of different materials: plants, of a chemical substance of three elements,- carbon, hydrogen, and oxygen; animals of one of four elements, nitrogen being added to the other three.

Asa Gray

I started Friends of Finn to raise money and awareness about the issue of puppy mills, which are illegal breeding facilities where animals are often bred to death and mistreated. It's a prevalent problem and a million dollar industry in the United States.

Amanda Hearst

We humans are here because nothing can be perfect. There always have to be some living things that are unsatisfied, itchy, trying too hard. If it was all just animals and rocks and lettuce, the gods wouldn't feel like they had enough to do.

Miranda July

The harming of animals for any reason is shameful, but torturing them for mere vanity is senseless. Slaughtering animals for their fur or harming them for cosmetic purposes is disgusting and not worth the perfect shade of lipstick.

Laura Mennell

I've always been fascinated by the way that children and animals suffer stoically in a way that I don't think adults do.

Rebecca Miller

When I'm not working, I love going to the beach. I am from Florida, so I definitely love the beach life. I love horse-back riding. Just to go out to a barn, it's fun. It's kind of like a get-away from the city. And also, I love animals.

Stefanie Scott

I love puppies, and I love animals in general. Besides that, I do martial arts: extreme martial arts. I also play real guitar and drums, and sing. And I'm taking some college classes, hoping to major in English and creative writing.

Cameron Monaghan

The 'here' of Watts is pastel houses with window gratings in curly patterns. 'Here' is yard sales with bins full of stuffed animals and used water guns. Here is Crips turf.

Leslie Jamison

I have had strange animals as pets all my life. I was shy growing up, and shy people tend to interact better with animals than people. Animals are direct, not duplicitous.

Yvonne Craig

My object will be, first, to show by what connections the history of the fossil bones of land animals is linked to the theory of the earth and why they have a particular importance in this respect.

Georges Cuvier

Secondly, the nature of the revolutions which have altered the surface of the earth must have had a more decisive effect on the terrestrial quadrupeds than on the marine animals.

Georges Cuvier

I'm a Taurus, which sounds like the name of a pickup truck. I'd prefer to be born under the sign of the rock wallaby. If you're going to interpret your life pursuant to an utterly irrational dogma, why can't it have a cute mascot? Rock wallabies really are fabulous animals, and in any remotely just world, they would have their own star sign.

Elliot Perlman

Although finding fruit flies in your wine or beer can be a bit annoying, I hope people will pause to admire the tenacity of these clever little creatures. They are really just hungry animals looking for something to eat, and have no intention of ruining your happy hour.

Michael Dickinson

If flies are a great model, they're a great model for flies. These animals, you know, they're not like us. We don't fly. We don't have a compound eye. I don't think we process sensory information the same way. The muscles that they use are just incredibly much more sophisticated and interesting than the muscles we use.

Michael Dickinson

They took their meals together; and it was remarked on
such occasions, when the friendship of animals is put to a
hard test, that they never quarrelled or disputed the
possession of a favourite fruit with each other.

Henry Walter Bates

There are good reasons why natural selection has become
widely accepted as an explanation of evolutionary
development. When applied to mammals and other large
animals, it fits perfectly. But we cannot assume that all
evolutionary steps arise from selection, particularly when
looking at smaller animals.

John Tyler Bonner

I look at trees, hunt mushrooms, and watch animals.
Fishing is what gets me out into the woods so I can notice
these things.

John D. Voelker

I had rather be an oyster than a man, the most stupid and
senseless of animals.

George Berkeley

The only meat I eat is from animals I've killed myself.

Mark Zuckerberg

We're in 'Jurassic Park' territory. If we go to the zoo in the future, we'll have zoos for extinct animals.

Michio Kaku

There the wild animals wandered and fed as though they were in a pasture that stretched much farther than a man could see, and there were no settlers. Only Indians lived there.

Laura Ingalls Wilder

Pray to Christ for me that the animals will be the means of making me a sacrificial victim for God.

Ignatius of Antioch

I talk to trees and animals. We have interesting conversations about food, weather, and love. They sometimes can predict the future.

Shan Sa

The cycle of life is death, decomposition and regeneration, and a person who wants to stop killing animals is actually anti-life because it's only in death that life can be regenerated.

Joel Salatin

I guess in general, people tend to not eat the cute animals.

Elayne Boosler

Grain that is used to feed animals that end up on our tables as turkeys and hams could have gone to feed starving people.

Peter Singer

Animals in the wild are lean, and I think we should be too.

Eddie Izzard

If you can kill animals, the same attitude can kill human beings. The mentality is the same which exploits nature and which creates wars.

Satish Kumar

Steve Irwin did wonderful conservation work but I was uncomfortable about some of his stunts. Even if animals aren't aware that you are not treating them with respect, the viewers are.

David Attenborough

Morality, as has often been pointed out, is antecedent to religion-it even exists in a rudimentary form among animals.

Herbert Read

If I hammer my own thumb while doing some DIY, it's not nice, but it's not the end of the world. To care obsessively about similar levels of discomfort in animals seems to be a case of mistaken moral priorities.

Julian Baggini

There is no doubt that there is a huge difference between human and nonhuman animals. But what we are overlooking is the fact that nonhuman animals are conscious beings, that they can suffer.

Peter Singer

Native Americans had only stone and wooden weapons and no animals that could be ridden. Those military advantages repeatedly enabled troops of a few dozen mounted Spaniards to defeat Indian armies numbering in the thousands.

Jared Diamond

My main issue is sustainability of the Earth, and protection of those animals and people who dwell here.

Lynda Resnick

You ask why I'm fascinated by the human figure? As a human animal, I am interested in some of my fellow animals: in their minds and bodies.

Lucian Freud

I knew there were, in myself, the souls of millions of people who lived centuries ago; not just people but animals, plants, the elements, things, even, matter. All of these exist in me.

Klaus Kinski

Some people are uncomfortable with the idea that humans belong to the same class of animals as cats and cows and raccoons. They're like the people who become successful and then don't want to be reminded of the old neighborhood.

Phil Donahue

I'm a vegetarian - I think there's a strong possibility, had I not become a vegetarian, I would not be working now. I became a vegetarian about 25 years ago, and I did it out of concern for animals. But I immediately began having more energy and feeling better.

Bob Barker

The features of globalization have huge consequences on pandemics. It just connects us so much more closely... And as a consequence, every one of these viruses that passes from animals to humans has the capacity to infect all of us.

Nathan Wolfe

There is something really mysterious about lions. They could rip you apart if they wanted to, but at the same time they look so cuddly. Can you imagine what humans look like to animals? They must think we're so weird.

Lee Ryan

One of my obsession is animals. I'm into dog rescues. It drives me crazy when people go to pet stores and buy dogs. There are so many dogs that need a good home. And this sounds crazy, but I really believe they know what is happening and are appreciative, and I just think they make for the best pets.

Jim O'Heir

I think what's great about your community is that it's different than anyone else's. Look around. What do you want to change? What needs to be built, or what's valuable and needs to be maintained? Is it the people? Local animals? Your parks or gardens? Hospitals?

Debby Ryan

Fork: An instrument used chiefly for the purpose of putting dead animals into the mouth.

Ambrose Bierce

The industrial food system is so cruel and so horrific in its treatment of animals. It never asks the question: 'Should a pig be allowed to express its pig-ness?'

Joel Salatin

Most sorts of diversion in men, children and other animals, are in imitation of fighting.

Jonathan Swift

Man, of all the animals, is probably the only one to regard himself as a great delicacy.

Jacques Yves Cousteau

We have wild animals in zoos, yet people rarely meet their 'food' face to face.

Elayne Boosler

I am opposed to the military use of animals. I am also opposed to the military use of men.

B. F. Skinner

Two of the many areas of conflict between Judeo-Christian values and leftism concern the separation between the holy and the profane and the separation between humans and animals.

Dennis Prager

Wouldn't it be great to see a line in all movie credits that truthfully says, 'Nobody was harmed in the making of this film, and at the cast party, all animals got a belly belly belly rub.'

Elayne Boosler

I looked about me once again, and suddenly the dancing horses without number changed into animals of every kind and into all the fowls that are, and these fled back to the four quarters of the world from whence the horses came, and vanished.

Black Elk

Cutting meat out of your diet is the best thing you can do for animals and your own health.

Joan Jett

We're highly social animals - I'm told by scientists that what makes us different from other animals is an acute social awareness, which is what has made us so successful.

Alan Alda

I cannot understand why any young man - or young woman, for that matter - would wish to undergo the painful process of disfiguring the skin with various multicolored representations of people, animals, and various symbols.

Gordon B. Hinckley

There is something basic about protecting land by taking it off the market. People should be able to enjoy where they live while at the same time protect the plants and animals around them.

Tom Hanks

At the end of the day, humans are social animals and we

are at our best when we get to do things with others who appreciate and enjoy what we enjoy. It's what keeps us human.

Simon Sinek

The behavior of men to the lower animals, and their behavior to each other, bear a constant relationship.

Herbert Spencer

Consciousness surely does not depend on language. Babies, many animals, and patients robbed of speech by brain damage are not insensate robots; they have reactions like ours that indicate that someone's home.

Steven Pinker

The older I get, the more individuality I find in animals and the less I find in humans.

Chuck Jones

You shouldn't say 'animals' to distinguish between humans and non-humans. We are all animals.

Peter Singer

Like most animals, we're wired to associate height with power.

Helen Fisher

Before I had my child, animals were my life. I slept with four dogs in my bed.

Salma Hayek

I really love animals and enjoy working with them.

Emma Watson

We're animals. We're born like every other mammal and we live our whole lives around disguised animal thoughts.

Barbara Kingsolver

We animals live life in all its glorious uncertainty. Why do politicians think they can control events?

Rita Mae Brown

There is that thing about not working with animals and children - I don't think that's true. Although you should never work with donkeys.

Emma Thompson

I love animals and feel very strongly that people should not be allowed to buy a pet if they are not able to look after it.

Kirsty Gallacher

In most of the world, it is accepted that if animals are to be killed for food, they should be killed without suffering.

Peter Singer

I don't like to see animals in pain. That was very uncomfortable to me. I don't like factory farming. I'm not an advocate for the meat industry.

Anthony Bourdain

I'm in the middle of my sixth book, which is about animals at the Los Angeles Zoo.

Betty White

As a biologist, I can't think of myself as anything but an animal among animals and plant.

Barbara Kingsolver

Spare a thought for the poor introverts among us. In a world of party animals and glad-handers, they're the ones who stand by the punch bowl. In a world of mixers and pub crawls, they prefer to stay home with a book. Everywhere around them, cell phones ring and e-mails chime and they just want a little quiet.

Jeffrey Kluger

Having my animals or my children with me exorcises that feeling of not being wanted.

Eartha Kitt

We created a line of pet food called Nutrish that's made to human standards, and 100 percent of the proceeds go to animal rescue. One of our top-tier donors is the ASPCA, and they help us challenge animal shelters all across the country to get more animals placed in homes.

Rachael Ray

In conditions of uncertainty, humans, like other animals, herd together for protection.

James Surowiecki

Human folk are as a matter of fact eager to find intelligence in animals.

Edward Thorndike

In 'We Were the Mulvaneys,' animals are almost as important as people. I wanted to show the tenderness in our relationships with cats, dogs, and horses. Especially cats.

Joyce Carol Oates

I like animals. I like natural history. The travel bit is not the important bit. The travel bit is what you have to do in order to go and look at animals.

David Attenborough

If we are concerned about the exploitation of human workers in countries with low standards of worker protection, we should also be concerned about the treatment of even more defenceless non-human animals.

Peter Singer

I've been bitten by a python. Not a very big one. I was being silly, saying: 'Oh, it's not poisonous...' Then, wallop! But you have fear around animals.

David Attenborough

I've worked with Morris Animal Foundation for more than 40 years now, and I'm so proud of all they've done to advance veterinary medicine for animals worldwide.

Betty White

We should all love animals.

Karl Pilkington

It is written in the Jewish law book, the Talmud, that only the Jew is human, that Gentiles are only animals.

Julius Streicher

From the lowest animals of which we can affirm intelligence up to man this type of intellect is found.

Edward Thorndike

We're animals. We're violent. We're criminal.

Maurice Sendak

I love animals.

Margaret Cho

Animals, or at least those who are conscious and capable of suffering or enjoying their lives, are not things for us to use in whatever way we find convenient.

Peter Singer

I have never really been fond of animals. I certainly wasn't an 'animal lover' when I became involved in the movement. I just came to be persuaded that animals should be treated as independent sentient beings, not as means to human ends.

Peter Singer

There is no excuse for keeping wild animals in amusement parks or circuses. Until our governments take action, we should avoid supporting places where captive wild animals perform for our amusement. If the public will not pay to see them, the businesses that profit from keeping animals captive will not be able to continue.

Peter Singer

I have yet to see one completely unspoiled star, except for the animals - like Lassie.

Edith Head

The proportion between the velocity with which men or animals move, and the weights they carry, is a matter of considerable importance, particularly in military affairs.

Charles Babbage

Animals, they are one of the most beautiful gifts we have and, you know, if there are people that have compassion, there are very few people that put their money into animal rescue organizations. And if there is someone that has that passion, animals need all the help they can get.

Alyssa Milano

History is a people's memory, and without a memory, man is demoted to the lower animals.

Malcolm X

If God did not intend for us to eat animals, then why did he make them out of meat?

John Cleese

Animation is different from other parts. Its language is the language of caricature. Our most difficult job was to develop the cartoon's unnatural but seemingly natural anatomy for humans and animals.

Walt Disney

I am personally not against keeping animals at zoos, as they serve a huge educational purpose, but treating them well and with respect seems the least we could do, and with 'we' I mean not just zoo staff, but most certainly also the public.

Frans de Waal

Burning carbon-based substances like oil, gas, and especially coal, produces billions of tons of extra carbon dioxide each year. Methane gas from cows and pigs and other animals on our large farms ends up in the atmosphere as well, trapping more of the sun's energy as heat.

Bill Nye

I like animals, all animals. I wouldn't hurt a cat or a dog - or a chicken or a cow. And I wouldn't ask someone else to hurt them for me. That's why I'm a vegetarian.

Peter Dinklage

Zoo animals are ambassadors for their cousins in the wild.

Jack Hanna

I like animals because they are not consciously cruel and don't betray each other.

Taylor Caldwell

The innocence of childhood is like the innocence of a lot of animals.

Clint Eastwood

As long as man continues to be the ruthless destroyer of lower living beings he will never know health or peace. For as long as men massacre animals, they will kill each other.

Pythagoras

The first day I walked into prison, and he slammed that door, I knew the magnitude of the decision that I made, and the poor judgment, and what I allowed to happen to the animals. And, you know, it's no way of explaining the hurt and the guilt that I felt. And that was the reason I cried so many nights.

Michael Vick

If everyone took personal responsibility for their animals, we wouldn't have a lot of the animal problems that we do. I'm a big spay-and-neuter supporter. Don't have babies if you're not going to take care of those babies. We don't need more. We just need to take care of the ones we have. Take responsibility and breathe kindness.

Betty White

The thing that differentiates man from animals is money.

Gertrude Stein

If you don't have imagination, you stop being human; animals don't have imagination; Alzheimer's is the death of imagination.

Devdutt Pattanaik

For better or worse, zoos are how most people come to know big or exotic animals. Few will ever see wild penguins sledding downhill to sea on their bellies, giant pandas holding bamboo lollipops in China or tree porcupines in the Canadian Rockies, balled up like giant pine cones.

Diane Ackerman

Animals don't lie. Animals don't criticize. If animals have moody days, they handle them better than humans do.

Betty White

The man who kills the animals today is the man who kills the people who get in his way tomorrow.

Dian Fossey

The propensity to truck, barter and exchange one thing for another is common to all men, and to be found in no other race of animals.

Adam Smith

It was wrong to capture wild animals and confine them in captivity for people to go and gawk at them. And that's basically how zoos got started. But once you do that, and once you have animals that have been bred in captivity, you're really stuck with them in some sense. You can't return them to the wild.

Peter Singer

Popular culture bombards us with examples of animals being humanized for all sorts of purposes, ranging from education to entertainment to satire to propaganda. Walt Disney, for example, made us forget that Mickey is a mouse, and Donald a duck. George Orwell laid a cover of human societal ills over a population of livestock.

Frans de Waal

You don't see sick animals in the wild. You don't see lame animals in the wild, and its all because of the predator: the lion, the tiger, the leopard, all the cats.

Tippi Hedren

Birth, life, death is a cycle. And they're all beautiful, you celebrate all of them. Animals do grieve, but they move on. That's the lesson behind animals.

Cesar Millan

Man is the only creature that consumes without producing. He does not give milk, he does not lay eggs, he is too weak to pull the plough, he cannot run fast enough to catch rabbits. Yet he is lord of all the animals.

George Orwell

I mean, I have done scenes with animals, with owls, with bats, with cats, with special effects, with thespians, in the freezing cold, in the pouring rain, boiling hot; I've done press with every syndication, every country; I've done interviews with people dressed up as cows - there's honestly nothing that's gonna intimidate me!

Emma Watson

Sharks are beautiful animals, and if you're lucky enough to see lots of them, that means that you're in a healthy ocean. You should be afraid if you are in the ocean and don't see sharks.

Sylvia Earle

The attitude we have towards our personal pets as opposed to the animals that suffer under the factory farm is hypocritical and delusional.

James Cromwell

I don't eat four-legged animals, but I eat birds, I eat cheese, I eat dessert. I eat everything.

Gwyneth Paltrow

God, that all-powerful Creator of nature and architect of the world, has impressed man with no character so proper to distinguish him from other animals, as by the faculty of speech.

Quintilian

For me, it always has to be about health. That's why I'm a

vegan. Well, I don't even do that for my health entirely, I do it for animals.

Emily Deschanel

People are powerfully moved by imagination, belief, and knowledge. They can consider the past and future. They can make changes in their behavior out of reason in a way that animals can't do.

Gretchen Rubin

The fashion industry has a responsibility to represent a healthy image of women, but to start weighing them and putting them against a wall and making them feel like animals? No.

Diane von Furstenberg

There will always be vain, obsessive people who want to own rare and extraordinary things whatever the cost; there will always be people for whom owning beautiful, dangerous animals brings a sense of power and magic.

Susan Orlean

Amongst the minds of animals that of man leads, not as a demigod from another planet, but as a king from the same race.

Edward Thorndike

For origin and development of human faculty we must look to these processes of association in lower animals.

Edward Thorndike

Everyone agrees that animals should not be exposed to unnecessary pain. But neither should scientists be hamstrung by the requirement to use anesthesia in every animal experiment that might cause pain.

Timothy Noah

In Tennessee where I grew up, there were animals, farms, wagons, mules.

Tina Turner

My own field, the prevention of genetic disorders in babies, has been possible only because of humane work on animals.

Robert Winston

We were playing a fair, and a few people were handing me stuffed animals and flowers, but one person handed me a paper sack. So I took all the stuff back to the bus. I put the sack in my lap and opened it, and a live iguana jumped out of the sack and onto my shirt. I screamed like a little girl!

Blake Shelton

I love that quiet time when nobody's up and the animals are all happy to see me.

Olivia Newton-John

I've dressed thousands of actors, actresses and animals, but whenever I am asked which star is my personal favorite, I answer, 'Grace Kelly.' She is a charming lady, a most gifted actress and, to me, a valued friend.

Edith Head

I'm a real animal lover. I adore animals of all shapes and sizes.

Tamsin Egerton

To me, it is one world, and the non-human animals bear the brunt of oppression and suffering.

Ingrid Newkirk

I used to swim with these beavers in a beaver pond when I was 10. I went back when I was 11 and found there were no more beavers. I found that trappers had taken them all, so I became quite angry, and that winter I began to walk the trap lines and free animals from the traps and destroy the traps.

Paul Watson

Whales are killed today to supply the limited demand for whale meat or to be used in pet foods or as fodder for fur-bearing animals used in the fur trade.

Paul Watson

I found myself compelled - like this weird, shameful compulsion - to draw cute animals.

Lynda Barry

Love can never make you weak, and love is not restricted to opposite sex. I love my parents, I love my animals, and I love my profession.

Randeep Hooda

Our expression and our words never coincide, which is why the animals don't understand us.

Malcolm de Chazal

Our instinctual understanding of reality is the same as most other animals.

Robert Lanza

For me, going vegan was an ethical and environmental decision. I'm doing the right thing by the animals.

Alexandra Paul

I couldn't date someone who didn't like dogs. There are exceptions to the rule, but I find that if someone doesn't like animals, I am a little suspicious of them.

Penn Badgley

My father was a really sharp cartoonist and filmmaker. He used to tape-record the family surreptitiously, either while we were driving around or at dinner, and in 1963 he and I made up a story about a brother and a sister, Lisa and Matt, having an adventure out in the woods with animals.

Matt Groening

It is up to the public to stop attending these theatrical, and aquatic shows, and circuses with wild animals. The rhetoric about how the animals are happy and well cared for are lies. Don't be swayed by them. The money behind these shows is huge; there is nothing good about them.

Tippi Hedren

I like animals. I like people who like animals. I hate people who love animals to the point they lose their sense of reason. I'm talking the 'my computer wallpaper is my dog,' 'I hang a Christmas stocking for my cat' crowd.

John Ridley

I love animals, always have, and it seemed natural to help the ASPCA. Animals have no voice of their own, so we have to be that voice.

Laurell K. Hamilton

Horseracing and ranch horses are two different animals. You're getting race horses out and running and running them. It can be really problematic. A thoroughbred's very delicate.

Dennis Quaid

My relaxation has always been my animals - going to the dog park with them, going to the beach.

Hilary Swank

Animal hoarding was a dirty secret until hoarders appeared on our TV screens and showed how they are compelled to collect so many dogs, cats or parrots that the animals end up in cages only inches bigger than their own bodies. For life.

Ingrid Newkirk

Everything that I've done in my life was to lead me to my work with the animals.

Tippi Hedren

I don't want food that comes from animals that are caged up and fed antibiotics. I am really suspicious of that kind of production of meat and poultry.

Alice Waters

Learn from nature. Stuff lives and stuff dies all the time, you know. Animals and birds and flowers. Trees come and go, and we come and go. That's it. So we should all seize life and make the most of what we have while we can.

Joanna Lumley

My mother early on taught us to respect all animals, and I mean all animals - not just cats and dogs but rats and snakes and spiders and fish and wildlife, so I really grew up believing they are just like us and just as deserving of consideration.

Joanna Lumley

We need a better way to talk about eating animals, a way that doesn't ignore or even just shruggingly accept things like habits, cravings, family and history but rather incorporates them into the conversation. The more they are allowed in, the more able we will be to follow our best instincts.

Jonathan Safran Foer

We need to separate the process of evolution - which is, indeed, a self-serving process - and the actual motivations of animals.

Frans de Waal

Human beings are social animals; we devote a significant portion of our brain just to dealing with interactions with other humans.

Jamais Cascio

Animals are everywhere. Some are more romantic, like tigers and elephants and chimpanzees, and some are less romantic, like earthworms, but they are just as interesting.

Isabella Rossellini

I have friends who are black, white, purple, gay, straight, Martian, yellow, old, and young. I have friends who are animals and a few who I believe to be robots. All of them are people to me. In my mind, it's not about what you look like or what you do; it's about who you are inside.

Tracy Morgan

The main peculiarity which distinguishes man from other animals is the means of his support-the power which he possesses of very greatly increasing these means.

Thomas Malthus

I live in New York, and the only live animals you see are cockroaches, rats and pigeons, which I admire immensely. When I see an animal that thrives in the garbage, I feel relief; in our urban environment, other animals are dying out.

Isabella Rossellini

I was always interested in animals, but when I was little, animal behavior was still a new science. It was available to become a veterinarian, it was available to study biology, but not specifically animal behavior. In the '60s, Jane Goodall was the founder of this new science.

Isabella Rossellini

Like many animals, wild ponies can sense a drop in barometric pressure. When a storm threatens, they know to seek shelter in hilly areas and huddle together with their rumps facing the oncoming wind.

Diane Ackerman

What a lonely species we are, searching for signals of life from other galaxies, adopting companion animals, visiting parks and zoos to commune with other beasts. In the process, we discover our shared identity.

Diane Ackerman

Humans are vulnerable, messy little animals and that's normal. And all I want to do is make a space for that in my films.

Mike Mills

Far too often animals are put to sleep when they could be saved through proper care and nursing.

Louis Leakey

We do not need to eat animals, wear animals, or use

animals for entertainment purposes, and our only defense of these uses is our pleasure, amusement, and convenience.

Gary L. Francione

The earth is a great big orphanage for most animals.

Eric Roberts

People are always the start for me... animals, when I can get into their heads, gods, supernatural beings, immortals, the dead... these are all people to me.

Tanith Lee

Man is an individual. The animals, plants and minerals are divided into species. They are not individualized in the same sense that man is.

Max Heindel

The beliefs I was raised with - to respect animals and to be aware of nature, to understand that we share this planet with other creatures - have had a huge impact on me.

Stella McCartney

Animals aren't any better equipped to survive an emergency than humans are. Few people missed the fact that after Hurricane Katrina, people died because buses and emergency shelters wouldn't allow their animals.

Ingrid Newkirk

One thing I think kids need to do is more chores, and take care of their own rooms. Responsibilities are really important to start them with. If they have animals, they have to feed them and care for them. That's the only way I think I could do it.

Faith Ford

After spending time with the rescued turkeys at Farm Sanctuary's shelter and seeing how similar they are to my furry companion animals at home, I knew I needed to do everything in my power to protect these friendly and curious birds from the daily pain and suffering they endure on factory farms.

Ginnifer Goodwin

I am in the process of starting a nonprofit organization that gives rescued animals a home in a simulated wild environment and, for those who have been tested on, who are disabled, aggressive, etc., their own space to live out their days.

Casey Affleck

I love animals, and I was always attracted to the idea of being a zoo veterinarian or a veterinarian with the circus.

Kay Redfield Jamison

In Africa, we have the bush meat trade, which means that, on a very large scale, animals are being killed in the forests and sold in the cities as a luxury food.

Frans de Waal

Sometimes I read about someone saying with great authority that animals have no intentions and no feelings, and I wonder, 'Doesn't this guy have a dog?'

Frans de Waal

When I go home, I play with my baby dolls and strollers and stuffed animals, pretend like they're real dogs.

Elle Fanning

Early experiences convinced me that animals can and do have quite distinct personalities.

Chuck Jones

Ever since 'Lassie' and 'Old Yeller', I won't watch animal movies. Animals in movies always die.

George A. Romero

The history of agriculture is the history of humans breeding seeds and animals to produce traits we want in our crops and livestock.

Michael Specter

In Yellowstone National Park, there are more 'do not feed the animals' signs than there are animals you might wish to feed.

Natalie Jeremijenko

I love looking after animals. I find it very enjoyable.

Paul O'Grady

We are the first to ever publicly advertise we don't test on animals.

John Paul DeJoria

I can't say I'm not guilty of age discrimination when it comes to animals. Like most people I've walked into a shelter more than a few times and a magnetic force has pulled me toward those fluffy little puppies in the corner cage.

Jenna Morasca

I am interested in 18th century natural philosophy, science, particularly botany, the study of hybridity in plants and animals, which, of course, then allows me to consider the hybridity of language.

Natasha Trethewey

My parents were very permissive when it came to animals. As long as we earned the money to buy them and built whatever structure it was they were going to live in, we could have any kind of pet we wanted. They would have let us have a rhinoceros if we could have afforded it.

Maggie Stiefvater

When I was a child I used to read books by Gerald Durrell, who founded Jersey Zoo. He had a job collecting animals for zoos and for a long time that is what I wanted to do. Later when I was a teenager I had a fantastic English teacher called Mrs. Stafford. Her enthusiasm made me decide to be a writer.

Melvin Burgess

Our children think our world will end. It's a tragic thing. Adults don't think that. They don't see that we are eating the planet. But we are. If you take all the biomass of vertebrates on the planet, 98% are men and their domestic animals. All the wild animals in the world make up only 2%.

Yann Arthus-Bertrand

Animals mean everything to me. We have to be their voice and protectors.

Shannon Elizabeth

I like using animals because they help suspend my reader's

disbelief. We have certain ideas about dentists. We don't have many ideas about rhinoceros dentists.

Yann Martel

Every literary culture has among its first bearings the 'blether' of animals who seek to make sense of human existence.

Andrew O'Hagan

The things that drive me crazy are coming from this place of people suffering because of people polluting into rivers or whatever. It's not simply just about systems; it's an emotional reaction to seeing animals or people suffering.

Mike White

But if you love animals for all the right reasons- and that's just love and affection- then you're going to go after animals who need you.

Eric Roberts

If all consciousness is subject to essential laws in a manner similar to that in which spatial reality is subject to mathematical laws, then these essential laws will be of most fertile significance in investigating facts of the conscious life of human and brute animals.

Edmund Husserl

All of us in society are supposed to believe that cruelty to animals is wrong and that it is a good thing to prevent needless suffering. So if that is true, how can meat be acceptable under any but the most extraordinary circumstances, such as perhaps roasting the bird who died flying into a window?

Ingrid Newkirk

There's nothing humane about the flesh of animals who have had one or two or even three improvements made in their singularly rotten lives on today's factory farms.

Ingrid Newkirk

Whether or not we are religious, respecting others should be seen as just as important as looking out for ourselves, yet it requires discipline to change our bad habits that cause pain to animals.

Ingrid Newkirk

I always wanted to be a zoologist. I'm fascinated with animals. I wanted to be a zookeeper.

Nigel Barker

When you write about animals, of course, you are really writing about the people who love and live with them. Animals mirror and reveal us. Dogs in particular are often reflections of us, and what we need them to be.

Jon Katz

But I'm very happy with my life the way it has been turning out. A little time in the country, a little time with the animals and working on behalf of them.

Mary Tyler Moore

New England waters are some of my favorite - they are some of the richest waters because they are temperate waters and nutrient-rich, and therefore provide food for so many animals, from giant whales to sharks to everything else.

Brian Skerry

I do not want to go into its physical reasons: the construction of the human body is different from that of carnivorous animals. But man's intelligence is such that it can be utilised to defend any-thing he does, whether right or wrong.

Morarji Desai

I think the moment that I'm very proud of is building a business without using animals. And, hopefully, changing people's perception of how you can do luxury fashion.

Stella McCartney

We're all just animals. That's all we are, and everything else is just an elaborate justification of our instincts. That's where music comes from. And romantic poetry. And bad novels.

Elvis Costello

Independence is all very well, but we animals never allow our friends to make fools of themselves beyond a certain limit; and that limit you've reached.

Kenneth Grahame

It's commonly said that if slaughterhouses had clear glass walls, nobody would eat meat. I think people go out of their way to remain ignorant about how factory farm animals are treated.

Steve-O

I think of animals more as spirits that come and go. They enter our lives at a particular time and they leave at a particular time. The whole glorious history of animals with people is about joy and connection. It's about loving this creature and letting this creature love you.

Jon Katz

The Animals were their own worst enemy. The Animals were a band that couldn't live up to their name. I was the singer in the band and as long as I was enjoying myself I would keep on working with the band. But it got to be rather nasty once the big money showed up - things started to turn toxic.

Eric Burdon

A lot of hip-hop artists wear fur, and they think it's a status symbol. That doesn't register for me; I just see dead animals.

Tommy Lee

But if you really want to learn about life, get a cat. The way I think people should relate to animals is with a cat. Because the world is his.

James Cromwell

There is no moral distinction between fur and other materials made from animals, such as leather, which also is the result of the suffering and death of sentient beings.

Gary L. Francione

The doctrine of marriage depends on Genesis being true. If there's an absolute authority, and if God's the Creator, He made one man and one woman. Jesus came and said that marriage is between a man and woman. If Genesis is not true, we're just animals, and marriage is just whatever you want to make it to be.

Ken Ham

My mother taught me a lot about respect for all living

things - for plants and animals. I am a vegetarian. I was
brought up that way.

David LaChapelle

I would like to do all kinds of things: photography and art
and designing; I want to help do charity things for animals
and things like that.

Georgia May Jagger

The minute that you bring a unicorn into a story, you know
that it's a fairy tale or a fable, because unicorns don't exist
as animals. They exist as fantasy creatures.

Gloria Vanderbilt

The holidays are also a time when people freak out about
their finances. If you don't want to spend the money, why
not try some of the other options instead of killing a bunch
of animals?

Christina Applegate

Without a notion of the transcendental, human beings
would, indeed, be animals; however, only fools can be

convinced of it, and only degenerates need such a
conviction.

Franz Grillparzer

All living beings, not just animals, but plants and
microorganisms, perceive. To survive, an organic being
must perceive - it must seek, or at least recognize, food and
avoid environmental danger.

Lynn Margulis

My whole background is character acting: weird costumes,
fat suits, playing men, playing animals - I've never played
anyone with whom there's any overlapping Venn diagram.

Allison Williams

Pet lovers know that animals sometimes understand us
better than we do, and the annals of human sin and desire
provide plenty of stories to drive the point home.

Tony Snow

Although native Africans domesticated some plants in the
Sahel and in Ethiopia and in tropical West Africa, they

acquired valuable domestic animals only later, from the north.

Jared Diamond

In all works on Natural History, we constantly find details of the marvellous adaptation of animals to their food, their habits, and the localities in which they are found.

Alfred Russel Wallace

I mean, I really don't want the federal government to be determining whether or not a person who feels certain ways about the environment or about animals or about certain religious issues should be considered an extremist. That to me is a type of thought control, mind control, which is very dangerous.

Peter T. King

Humans are something very different from animals, and the numbers required to get cloning to work in animals are completely prohibitory with humans.

Christiane Nusslein-Volhard

Now that I know how supermarket meat is made, I regard eating it as a somewhat risky proposition. I know how those animals live and what's on their hides when they go to slaughter, so I don't buy industrial meat.

Michael Pollan

When I was a very young author, I knew I needed to build myself a tower outside of Europe. Like when you're a hunter, and build towers to watch the animals move. I knew I would never understand the world without that perspective. I came to Africa for that rational reason, although I love Mozambique now.

Henning Mankell

I suppose I am one: an activist - for animals and a vegan lifestyle. I hear that word, however, and look around to see if someone is indeed referring to me.

Victoria Moran

The nature of human beings is to eat meat and fruits and vegetables, and therefore we have to kill animals. I don't have a problem with that. But it's a sacred moment. It's a gift of life.

Eric Ripert

Cruelty to men and to the lower animals as well, which would have passed unnoticed a century ago, now shocks the sensibilities and is regarded as wicked and degrading.

Elihu Root

I'm going to be doing exactly what I'm doing now - teaching people about animals.

Bindi Irwin

It's about keeping animals in our environment. They can't be on somebody's purse or shoes or something.

Bindi Irwin

Working on behalf of companion animals is so important. We start to realize how healing they are.

Bernadette Peters

I love pets and I love animals, and I just got a new puppy, a new rescue named Peanut. She's a tiny little Chihuahua mix.

Carrie Ann Inaba

When it comes to wilderness animals we have to make an effort to preserve what areas we can that they can be themselves in. Its come to a point though, clearly, where some species have to be cared for by humans if they are not going to disappear altogether.

Matthew Fox

I love dogs, horses and generally all animals.

Jacqueline Winspear

If a horse doesn't want to do something, you're not going to make him do it. They're incredibly powerful animals.

Jeremy Irvine

Slowly, but with no doubt or hesitation whatever, and in something of a solemn expectancy, the two animals passed through the broken tumultuous water and moored their boat at the flowery margin of the island.

Kenneth Grahame

We humans have a tendency to see ourselves as completely different from other animals, and the way in which large segments of the public continue to reject the theory of evolution is just one symptom of that malaise.

Kenneth R. Miller

Rather than studying the most complex form of memory in a very complicated animal, we had to take the most simple form - an implicit form of memory - in a very simple animal. So I began to look around for very simple animals. And I focused in on the marine snail Aplysia.

Eric Kandel

Animal-rights advocates remind us of this admonition: The ways in which people treat animals will be reflected in how people relate to one another.

William Greider

The ways in which people treat animals will be reflected in how people relate to one another.

William Greider

I grew up with lots of animals and I related more to them than I did to people. I feel a lot of empathy for them.

Neko Case

Our success was mainly due to the fact that we stimulated the nerves of animals that easily stood on their own feet and were not subjected to any painful stimulus either during or immediately before stimulation of their nerves.

Ivan Pavlov

When I was 18 I worked with the Ringling Brothers circus, taking care of menagerie animals. I used to rather deliberately risk my life with the big cats.

Edward Hoagland

.

Biology will relate every human gene to the genes of other animals and bacteria, to this great chain of being.

Walter Gilbert

Thousands of years ago, humans domesticated every possible large wild mammal species fulfilling all those criteria and worth domesticating, with the result that there have been no valuable additions of domestic animals in recent times, despite the efforts of modern science.

Jared Diamond

It has been generally the custom of writers on natural history to take the habits and instincts of animals as the fixed point, and to consider their structure and organization as specially adapted to be in accordance with them.

Alfred Russel Wallace

Growing up human is uniquely a matter of social relations rather than biology. What we learn from connections within the family takes the place of instincts that program the behavior of animals; which raises the question, how good are these connections?

Elizabeth Janeway

Basically, the reason I'm vegan is because when I was about 16 or 17 years old, I began to understand that we don't need to contribute to the killing and exploitation of animals to feed our bodies correctly.

Daniel Johns

Cats aren't cooperative in the same way that other animals are. You can train a dog to act, but you can't train a cat in the same way.

Michael Showalter

We're all animals, but we're a different sort of animal. Maybe they're better than us. They're more loyal. They're more pure. They're more simple. They're not neurotic. Well, there are some neurotic dogs.

Kevin Kline

Evolution explains our biological evolution, but human beings are very unique creatures. As the Dobzhansky said, all animals are unique; humans are the uniquest. And that uniqueness of being human, language, art, culture, our dependency on culture for survival, comes from the combination of traditional biological evolution.

Donald Johanson

It is in his knowledge that man has found his greatness and his happiness, the high superiority which he holds over the other animals who inhabit the earth with him, and consequently no ignorance is probably without loss to him, no error without evil.

James Smithson

You can draw the character out of pets, and you can make them your friends, but they are animals, and they have to be allowed to live the lives of animals.

Paul O'Grady

We're not just social animals in the conventional way that people think. It's not just a bunch of us who hang out together. We have a very specific pattern of ties, and they have a particular shape and structure that is encoded in our genes. It means that human beings have evolved to live their lives embedded in social networks.

Nicholas A. Christakis

Just as predatory animals follow a similar general design and behave in similar ways, so organizations, especially those in competition with one another, must follow certain design principles if they are to succeed and prevail.

Robert Shea

Nothing to be done really about animals. Anything you do looks foolish. The answer isn't in us. It's almost as if we're put here on earth to show how silly they aren't.

Russell Hoban

Of all living things, only humans consciously anticipate death; the consequent need to choose how to behave in its face - to worry about how to die - distinguishes us from other animals. The need to manage death is the particular lot of humanity.

Drew Gilpin Faust

All comic books take place in built environments, and I was very good at drawing people and animals, and stuff like that, but I hadn't spent much energy drawing buildings. So I thought, maybe I could, and then I became an architect.

Bjarke Ingels

I'm trying to get across the message that don't be afraid of animals, they're just put on this earth to help the environment and everything like that.

Bindi Irwin

Animals speak with pure affection. It's important to me to get something going in NY so we can get to be a no-kill city, and give the animals homes and more attention and love.

Bernadette Peters

Life evolved under conditions of light and darkness, light and then darkness. And so plants and animals developed their own internal clocks so that they would be ready for these changes in light. These are chemical clocks, and they're found in every known being that has two or more cells and in some that only have one cell.

Jessa Gamble

I like to do chill things on dates. I think it would be fun to go to the zoo. I know it's really weird and random, but I love animals. It'd be like a day of doing silly things, while enjoying nature.

Ashlee Simpson

I was so sad from losing two of my dogs and my mother. I had this vision of all these animals sitting behind bars. They had no control and were scared. That's why I got into fostering and adopting animals out.

Linda Blair

The animals are right here, right in front of us. And how we treat these companions is a test.

Linda Blair

I laughed when Steven Spielberg said that cloning extinct animals was inevitable. But I'm not laughing anymore, at least about mammoths. This is going to happen. It's just a matter of working out the details.

Hendrik Poinar

After I recovered from 'Lioness', I wanted to write something about animals because I really like mythical creatures, especially dragons. At 12, I was one of those semi-recluses who did better with animals than people. Out of that, came the character, Daine, who could communicate with animals.

Tamora Pierce

I accredit animals for keeping me going when times were bad.

Kelly Bishop

The information that is passed from person to person and from generation to generation is the primary factor that gives humans a competitive advantage over other animals.

Keith Henson

I have a huge passion for animals and while retirement is a long way off, when I do I would love to do something with animals.

Sally Pearson

Swine flu is not an anomaly. We know that swine flu - like the vast majority of new outbreaks - comes from animals. We should be monitoring those animals and the humans that come into contact with them, so we can catch these viruses early, before they infect major cities and spread throughout the world.

Nathan Wolfe

We had a small farm growing up. It was my grandfather's farm, and we didn't torture the animals, and we didn't feed them stuff we wouldn't eat.

Sandra Lerner

Animals have always been a passion of mine, being able to help them because they can't help themselves, and I think that people have treated them so badly over the years and it's just not fair. It's something I feel like I can help make a difference.

Shannon Elizabeth

I love living with animals. And my children love animals. I love walking around and being with the horses. But the deer? They're naughty.

Stephanie Seymour

Animals in general have sparked a weird depression in me, because as much as I tried, I couldn't layer a personality over them. You know what I mean? I would stare at the cows, and I would sing to the cows, and they would always just look at me blankly.

Kristen Schaal

I make skeletons that are able to walk on the wind, so they don't have to eat... eventually I want to put these animals out in herds on the beaches, so they will live their own lives.

Theo Jansen

In a way, Strandbeests have turned into migration animals, and the step counter gives them an idea of where they are. While counting their steps, they know more or less where they are between Kijkduin and Scheveningen.

Theo Jansen

Making lasting gifts for animals in our estate plans is perhaps the single most important thing we can do to ensure animals have the strongest possible voice for their protection.

Bea Arthur

It's been argued that of all the animals humans have domesticated, the horse is the most important to our history. For thousands of years, horses were our most reliable mode of transportation.

Elton Gallegly

I think some women try to make you feel you're not all female because you haven't given birth. There are a lot of prejudices. Some women think women who have animals are deeply sad, because what they really want is a child. Mind you, there's probably an element of truth in that.

Alison Goldfrapp

Elephants love to play around. They are very intelligent animals. They have a strong bond, at times stretching to several decades, with their mahouts.

Mark Shand

For decades I have tried to peel back the layers of mystery surrounding many marine creatures, though most have held tightly to their secrets. One animal that keeps me pondering is the shark. Spellbound by these enigmatic animals since I first encountered them in New England, I never tire of watching their special blend of power and grace.

Brian Skerry

An animal that is very abundant, before it gets extinct, it becomes rare. So you don't lose abundant animals. You always lose rare animals. Therefore, they're not perceived as a big loss.

Daniel Pauly

By exercising your stomach muscles, you wring out the body, you don't catch colds, you don't get cancer, you don't get hernias. Do animals get hernias? Do animals go on diets?

Joseph Pilates

I got into animals by drawing hair follicles. I liked drawing hair, and from that I got into feathers and fur, then into images of animals. The patterning is the same, but the proportions of the body change from one animal to the next. A lot of it is just geometry and consciousness.

Kiki Smith

Just because you're down to your last strike, you're not out yet. You can always do more. You'll always have more at-bats to take. That's true in baseball, in rescuing animals, and in life, generally.

Tony La Russa

It was always understood that plants and animals, though completely contrasted in their higher representatives, approached each other very closely in their lower and simpler forms. But they were believed not to blend.

Asa Gray

Animals are very easy to love and be friends with.

Stefanie Powers

I had given up magic, because it had reached a state of perfection. I felt that I was able to transform men into animals. I did not make use of this capability, because I believed I could not justify an intervention of this kind in the life of another person.

Wolfgang Hildesheimer

Pet stores just sell their animals.

Booboo Stewart

I'm a real pushover for animals.

Kevin Kline

Nothing can be more obvious than that all animals were created solely and exclusively for the use of man.

Thomas Love Peacock

People think if you have deciphered the genome of humans that you can change everything. But you cannot change everything, because you do not know what the genes mean, and you have no methods for changing them, and you can't do experiments with humans like you can with animals.

Christiane Nusslein-Volhard

I mean, I have done scenes with animals, with owls, with bats, with cats, with special effects, with thespians, in the freezing cold, in the pouring rain, boiling hot; I've done press with every syndication, every country; I've done interviews with people dressed up as cows - there's honestly nothing that's gonna intimidate me!

Emily Watson

Horses are prey animals, and most of the other animals that I've shot are predators. If you act mellow with predators, they know that they can kill you, so they are cool, but if you work with prey, they think that you're going to kill them at any moment.

Jill Greenberg

Actually, I don't like dogs. I'm from Morocco, and people there don't like animals.

Gad Elmaleh

When I was a kid if I was unhappy, I'd stroke my dog. I was into bringing injured birds into the house, RSPCA activities. And the relationship that you have with animals, you can get that from your children: that unquestioning love and adoration and equal need.

Steve McFadden

Animals are thinking, feeling creatures. They're sensitive.

Loretta Swit

I was raised in a strict Southern household in Lexington, South Carolina, and I remember sneaking off to watch 'Pet Cemetery' as a kid. After seeing those animals reincarnate, I screamed and couldn't sleep for weeks, but watched it again and again.

Jessica Stroup

Great Britain had a much different situation than we do and did here in the United States, in that they had literally thousands of infected animals with human health risks. Their infectivity in this disease happened before very much was known about it.

Ann Veneman

Besides alligators, the only animals to be feared are the poisonous serpents. These are certainly common enough in the forest, but no fatal accident happened during the whole time of my residence.

Henry Walter Bates

I'm impressed with how professional they are and what they can get an animal to do. I mean, dogs and cats - that's one thing. But when you get into the larger animals, that's a different thing all together.

M. Emmet Walsh

There is increasing social concern about our use of nonhumans for experiments, food, clothing and entertainment. This concern about animals reflects both our own moral development as a civilization and our recognition that the differences between humans and animals are, for the most part, differences of degree and not of kind.

Gary L. Francione

Everybody thinks people who promote PETA don't eat meat, but I think animals were made to be eaten.

Dominique Swain

Well, my life is so centered around the people I care about, my animals, and my work.

Bruce Weber

Like all animals, human beings have always taken what they want from nature. But we are the rogue species. We are unique in our ability to use resources on a scale and at a speed that our fellow species can't.

Edward Burtynsky

I really loved animals when I was little - my friend and I had an imaginary vet's office; we would mime doing surgery on animals. We treated more injuries than illnesses

- fixing with a baby bear with a broken leg, removing a tumor. Of course, our surgeries would take about five seconds; that's how good we were.

Hannah Murray

Factory farming came about from a moral race to the bottom, with corporations vying against each other to produce more and bigger animals with less care at lower cost.

Matthew Scully

Hence the same instant which killed the animals froze the country where they lived. This event was sudden, instantaneous, without any gradual development.

Georges Cuvier

My first attempts to transmit typhus to laboratory animals, including the smaller species of monkeys, had failed, as had those of my predecessors, for reasons which I can easily supply today.

Charles Jules Henry Nicole

What's the reality of being inside a zoo, for the animals and for the people who love and care for those animals? There's a lot of joy, and there's a lot of loss.

Thomas French

My wife says that I become different once I start to work with animals. My movements become different, my mood is different. It involves letting everything fall behind you, becoming intuitive in your dealings with wild creatures in a way that bypasses reason. Sometimes it's more like a dance than anything else.

Frans Lanting

I've had encounters with animals that have been really mystical. I've always been really into animals. But the way they appear in the paintings, they come from my mind's eye more than: 'I'm gonna draw a dog now.' It isn't thought out: "Now I'm gonna draw a bird.' They just appear.

John Lurie

I'll never stop eating animals, I'm sure, but I do think that for the benefit of everyone, the time has come to stop raising them industrially and stop eating them thoughtlessly.

Mark Bittman

One of the mistakes I made was thinking chickens and penguins could sing, just like all the other animals in the 'Muppets.' But it turns out those animals are not allowed to sing words.

Bret McKenzie

We should find inspiration in the senses that already exist and try to copy them and apply them to us. If we compare our senses to the senses of other animals and species that we don't have, we can get ideas for new abilities that we can adapt to humans by applying cybernetics to the body.

Neil Harbisson

I have a passion for animals and spend a lot of my spare time working with various organizations here in Toronto.

Lara Jean Chorostecki

I wish that the circuses that were around now felt like they did then. They're not quite as elegant or as magical as they used to be. There was something about the old tent shows, the Big Top, the canvas, the lights, the sawdust, the hay and the animals that's just missing now. Now, it's all urbanized and maybe a little garish.

Francis Lawrence

I've always wanted to work with dogs, so in high school, I worked at the Humane Society for a little while. I honestly think, even today, that would be the other career I would go into. Somehow I would be involved with animals.

Maggie Lawson

I am very fussy; I am very detailed; I nag a lot. So in a sense, I am like Mr. Ping. I am temperamental, I am emotional, I'm fussy, and I'm very exact. And I want people to not fail; I want them to execute - all those things Mr. Ping wants in other people. Or animals.

James Hong

People idealise their animals, and at the same time they patronisingly overlook a dog's natural life - biting fleas, burying bones, rolling in garbage, barking up an empty tree all night... But what do they do themselves? Bury stuff that will rot in secret and then dig it up and bury it again and rant and rave under empty trees!

Tove Jansson

I thought I was going to be a veterinarian. I was good in science and in math, and I loved animals.

Terry J. Lundgren

Science attempts to analyze how things and people and animals behave; it has no concern whether this behavior is good or bad, is purposeful or not. But religion is precisely the quest for such answers: whether an act is right or wrong, good or bad, and why.

Warren Weaver

I'm a huge animal lover - I love animals to death. I've got tortoises and three dogs, and I've had a million animals in the past. I just think that we should do all we can to take care of them.

Roshon Fegan

Any object, whether animate or inanimate, will have a size. Airplanes, boats, or musical string instruments vary in size just like animals and plants, and in all cases, their size and their material construction are totally different matters even though they affect one another.

John Tyler Bonner

Everything I do is to support my passion, and that is the rescuing of animals!

William McNamara

They are the most fascinating, intelligent, resourceful, adaptable animals I have ever seen. Grizzlies are a real symbol of true wildness.

Jim Cole

What do I mean when I say 'suspended animation'? It is the process by which animals de-animate, appear dead and then can wake up again without being harmed. OK, so here is the sort of big idea: If you look out at nature, you find that as you tend to see suspended animation, you tend to see immortality.

Mark Roth

I stopped eating beef in high school, and in college I stopped eating poultry. I am not a huge fan of factory farming and what we're doing to animals. I try to eat as clean as possible because I want to know what I'm putting into my body.

Susanna Thompson

Keep fighting for animals by making compassionate, cruelty-free choices every day and encouraging those around you to do the same.

Bea Arthur

If you're buying animal products and can go to the farm and actually see how the animals are looked after, yes, that's an important point. That's definitely the best way of assuring yourself that the animals are being well treated.

Peter Singer

Saving animals is as simple as choosing synthetic alternatives instead of real fur.

Natalie Imbruglia

First there was the theatre of people and animals, then of people and the devil. Now we need the theatre of people and people.

Edward Bond

Maybe one day the world will change, that we'll be in a luxurious position of being able to debate whether or not it's inherently wrong to eat animals, but the question doesn't matter right now.

Jonathan Safran Foer

All too often, academic departments defend their territory with the passion of cornered animals, though with far less justification.

Bruce Jackson

Being asked to support humane meat means being asked to support the suffering of animals in transport, to approve of treatment that causes them palpable fear, their bodies shaking and their eyes wide as saucers, as they are slung by their legs into crates that are slammed onto the back of a truck.

Ingrid Newkirk

I was sort of on a mission with 'American Splendor.' I wanted to try to prove that comics could do things. I wanted to expand them beyond superheroes and talking animals. And I knew that was going to take a long time.

But I just started writing an autobiography about my quotidian life.

Harvey Pekar

It's natural canine behavior to chew on all sorts of things, roll in other animals' droppings, hump and fight other dogs, menace anything that invades the home. All these behaviors can be curbed, but that takes a lot of work. Trainers say it requires nearly 2,000 repetitions of a behavior for a dog to completely absorb it.

Jon Katz

I go in the butchers and there's not a lot of meat I can eat these days, with having all the animals.

Paul O'Grady

I have always brought home stray animals - everything from squirrels to wild rabbits to foxes and turtles.

Amy Weber

Materialist philosophies that treat human beings as machines or animals possess the high ground in our culture

- academia, the most powerful media and many of our courts.

Marvin Olasky

Even if it had not been possible to reproduce the disease in animals and consequently to verify the hypothesis, this simple observation would have been sufficient to demonstrate the way in which the disease was propagated.

Charles Jules Henry Nicole

Animals are a continuous source of inspiration and wonder to me. I would love to play a dog.

James Ransone

Genomic science, as the newest frontier in scholarly research, is throwing open the door to a revolutionary way of approaching our health, the health and welfare of animals, and the sustainability of our environment.

John Sharp

Working with real wolves has been exhilarating. They're so amazing. They're these beautiful, brilliant animals and they're great to work with.

Kelly Overton

It must be the Brit in me, because I like animals.

Clint Eastwood

Animals often strike us as passionate machines.

Eric Hoffer

Without civilization, we would not turn into animals, but vegetables.

Mason Cooley

Becoming a grandmother brought me back to the things I forgot to love. Nature. Playing. Seeing animals. A new way of looking. A rejuvenation. A cycle of life - things come back to you. The details.

Carine Roitfeld

It's part of our pop culture to give animals human

personalities and talents.

Neil deGrasse Tyson

I personally cannot tell you how many times we rescuers put our names on animals to come to us as soon as they are eligible for release, only to find they have been senselessly killed by overzealous pound workers.

Elayne Boosler

It's been my dream to have four babies by 30. I look after animals, so I'd have a lot to give my kids.

Paris Hilton

I can't wait to have kids one day. I want to have kids and a farm with lots of animals on a lake.

Kirsten Dunst

I can no longer walk. I can no longer swim. But I'm lucky when I see how animals suffer.

Brigitte Bardot

I stopped making films to look after animals.

Brigitte Bardot

Human beings are religious animals.

Umberto Eco

Animals were my pets, and the thought of eating my pets freaked me out.

Carrie Underwood

No animal on the face of the earth could conceive of taxation. You and I work roughly six months a year to pay our local, state and federal taxes. If nothing else, this should convince you that animals are smarter than people.

Rita Mae Brown

I always had cats and animals, so children were never really in my thoughts.

Jacqueline Bisset

Mainly I'm a vegan because I like animals, and I don't want to be involved in their suffering. Also, it's better for my health and for the environment.

Moby

I like all these little animals that run and eat and hide all the time. I like their faces, They seem to be scared and curious at the same time.

Catherine Deneuve

We're not very dangerous animals; we don't have a horn like a rhino or quills like a porcupine.

Helen Fisher

I'm not a propagandist, I'm not a polemicist; my primary interest is just looking at and trying to understand how animals work.

David Attenborough

I love animals and I love working with them because they don't lie.

David Duchovny

Those who actually hate animals to the point of being cruel to them are outcasts to the rest of us, no matter where in the world they live.

Nick Clooney

In their sympathies, children feel nearer animals than adults.

Jessamyn West

As you may know, some of the stereotyped behaviors exhibited by autistic children are also found in zoo animals who are raised in a barren environment.

Temple Grandin

God sleeps in the minerals, awakens in plants, walks in animals, and thinks in man.

Arthur Young

The only way to save a rhinoceros is to save the environment in which it lives, because there's a mutual dependency between it and millions of other species of both animals and plants.

David Attenborough

Humans are amphibians - half spirit and half animal. As spirits they belong to the eternal world, but as animals they inhabit time.

C. S. Lewis

I think that intelligence is such a narrow branch of the tree of life - this branch of primates we call humans. No other animal, by our definition, can be considered intelligent. So intelligence can't be all that important for survival, because there are so many animals that don't have what we call intelligence, and they're surviving just fine.

Neil deGrasse Tyson

We are animals, born from the land with the other species. Since we've been living in cities, we've become more and more stupid, not smarter. What made us survive all these hundreds of thousands of years is our spirituality; the link to our land.

Sebastiao Salgado

People are not going to care about animal conservation unless they think that animals are worthwhile.

David Attenborough

Lions, wolves, and vultures don't live together in herds, droves or flocks. Of all animals of prey, man is the only sociable one. Every one of us preys upon his neighbor, and yet we herd together.

John Gay

Man is the most intelligent of the animals - and the most silly.

Diogenes

My mother and dad were big animal lovers, too. I just don't know how I would have lived without animals around me. I'm fascinated by them - both domestic pets and the wild community. They just are the most interesting things in the world to me, and it's made such a difference in my lifetime.

Betty White

Most people know that forests are the lungs of our planet,

literally playing a critical role in every breath we take. And that they're also home to incredible animals like the orangutan and elephant, which will go extinct if we keep cutting down their forests.

Chris Noth

It's important to remember that the animals are not grieving with us. They're very accepting. They're not lying there thinking 'How could you do this to me? Why aren't you keeping me going?' Pets don't do the human things of guilt and anger and recrimination that we do. They come and go with great acceptance.

Jon Katz

All animals, except man, know that the principal business of life is to enjoy it.

Samuel Butler

We'll lose more species of plants and animals between 2000 and 2065 than we've lost in the last 65 million years. If we don't find answers to these problems, we're gonna be victims of this extinction event that we're at fault for.

Paul Watson

Animals have a much better attitude to life and death than we do. They know when their time has come. We are the ones that suffer when they pass, but it's a healing kind of grief that enables us to deal with other griefs that are not so easy to grab hold of.

Emmylou Harris

When I look back over my life it's almost as if there was a plan laid out for me - from the little girl who was so passionate about animals who longed to go to Africa and whose family couldn't afford to put her through college. Everyone laughed at my dreams. I was supposed to be a secretary in Bournemouth.

Jane Goodall

Animals are something invented by plants to move seeds around. An extremely yang solution to a peculiar problem which they faced.

Terence McKenna

I became a vegetarian after I became aware of factory farming and slaughterhouses and the torture and inhumane handling of all these animals.

Kevin Nealon

I'm very caring with animals. I think patience is a big deal, because animals are always jumping around. I love to take care of people, so I think I'd be a good vet. I always wanted to be a vet when I was little.

Jennifer Love Hewitt

Man and animals are in reality vehicles and conduits of food, tombs of animals, hostels of Death, coverings that consume, deriving life by the death of others.

Leonardo da Vinci

People's hearts are like wild animals. They attach their selves to those that love and train them.

Ali ibn Abi Talib

I wish people would realize that animals are totally dependent on us, helpless, like children, a trust that is put upon us.

James Herriot

If a man lets all of my dogs sleep in the bed with us, then that is the most romantic thing. You must love my dogs in order to love me. A man who is nice to my animals and doesn't shoo them away - well, that's the height of romance.

Salma Hayek

Courage and conviction are powerful weapons against an enemy who depends only on fists or guns. Animals know when you are afraid; a coward knows when you are not.

David Seabury

Based on the Bible, I believe that all the land animals were made on day six, and Adam and Eve were made on day six, and people try to make fun of us for believing that dinosaurs lived with people, but there are a lot of animals living today that evolution says lived with dinosaurs.

Ken Ham

Keeping animals, I have learned, is all about water. Who even knew chickens drank water? I didn't, but they do, and a lot.

Susan Orlean

We're all animals.

John Malkovich

There is little evidence that other animals judge the appropriateness of actions that do not directly affect themselves.

Frans de Waal

I'm very touched on a deep level by cruelty to animals.

Ali MacGraw

States should pass laws making it illegal to own or trade wild animals; the phony 'educational' permits that many private owners have used to skirt those laws should be eliminated.

Susan Orlean

I might get some more animals or something, but I'm done with the kids. I got a boy, I got a girl, and I got an older boy. I'm straight.

Jada Pinkett Smith

It's funny what actors take issue with. Some won't do parts where animals are in jeopardy; some won't ever play anyone remotely unlikable - 'Heroes only, please.' Some won't do violence. I have no such qualms.

Rob Lowe

Having animals in the city is entirely different from having animals out in the country. For one thing, it's more social. When you live on lots of acres without neighbors within a stone's throw, your dog-walks are usually solitary rambles over hill and dale.

Susan Orlean

I try to do things that I think are helpful to the environment, to the animals, and to the planet.

Russell Simmons

Nearly all of the major kinds of life, divisions of life, phyla of animals, occur in the sea. Only about half of them can make it to land or freshwater.

Sylvia Earle

I love animals and they're very easy to look after when they're dead.

Amanda Seyfried

When I hear so-called professional journalists ask why we have celebrities speak for us and for the animals, the environment or social causes, I marvel at their denial of the rules of their own trade.

Paul Watson

You can now modify the genes of large animals, and the largest animal we are concerned with is the human.

Robert Winston

Ever since I was a little girl, I have always loved animals and been fascinated with them.

Isabella Rossellini

I was born with a love of animals, the same way I was born with brown hair. When I was a little girl in Rome, I always had pets, which I adored.

Isabella Rossellini

Future benefits rarely figure in the minds of animals.

Frans de Waal

Comedians and impressionists used to be two different showbiz animals entirely, but now there's no such thing as a comedian who doesn't do impressions.

John Podhoretz

If you want to look at the state of humans, you should look at the state of animals first. People are choosing whether or not they can feed an animal and their family. And every shelter coast-to-coast is stuffed.

Rachael Ray

I have no neighbours other than animals and Joshua Trees.

Don Van Vliet

I think there's a supreme power behind the whole thing, an intelligence. Look at all of the instincts of nature, both animals and plants, the very ingenious ways they survive. If you cut yourself, you don't have to think about it.

Clyde Tombaugh

If it is indeed impossible - or at least very difficult - to inhabit the consciousness of an animal, then in writing about animals there is a temptation to project upon them feelings and thoughts that may belong only to our own human mind and heart.

J. M. Coetzee

Bolivia recently did what every country should do - banned the use of animals in circuses.

Jane Velez-Mitchell

Using animals for entertainment is big business, plain and simple.

Jane Velez-Mitchell

Giraffes are fairytale animals, almost heraldic - as if from the land of fables. They have extremely beautiful faces, huge eyes, very sensitive nostrils and oh, blue tongues!

Joanna Lumley

Way back in the 1970s, I was eating a steak, and I looked down, and for the first time it suddenly looked like flesh to me - like a dead creature. In a flash, I realized that every time I ate any kind of meat, something had been killed for me, and I stopped eating all animals, not just cows and pigs but chickens and fish.

Joanna Lumley

Any time you're working in the world of taming animals, you're going to get hurt. But it's a rush that we get.

Cesar Millan

A book and a movie are different animals. You need a cinematic perspective to be involved in the motion pictures. And this is something I lack.

Ashwin Sanghi

There's a long tradition in Western thought that humans are not shackled by biology, whereas animals are pure instinct machines.

Frans de Waal

Ninety-five percent of the eggs produced in America come from factory-farmed birds. Even if free-range farms were hugely more humane, the sheer number of animals raised to satisfy people's desire for eggs, meat, and milk makes it impossible for us to raise them all on small, free-range farms.

Ingrid Newkirk

I first became a vegetarian when I was nine, in response to an argument made by a radical babysitter. My great change - which lasted a couple of weeks - was based on the very simple instinct that it's wrong to kill animals for food.

Jonathan Safran Foer

I know lots and lots and lots of vegetarians who think it's perfectly all right to kill animals for food to eat, but don't do it because they think all the ways in which it's done are wrong.

Jonathan Safran Foer

We're social animals. We've got to get along together. It's

in our nature. We're hardwired that way.

Nick Nolte

When you meet the farmers and go to the farms, you see that they treat their animals like they're family. It makes a big difference.

David Chang

At PETA, we often say that the issue of how animals are treated isn't just about them; it's about us, how we behave.

Ingrid Newkirk

I always dreamed when I was a little girl interested in animals that I would go live in Africa. Then I found out that you can look in your backyard, and you can do your own safari.

Isabella Rossellini

I grew up in a family of filmmakers, so I always wanted to make films about animals, especially comical films. Something about animals amuses me. And they have a great mystery. It's the same mystique some people might feel looking at the stars or the ocean.

Isabella Rossellini

I think I was always interested in animals. If a man likes a woman, you know, he might discuss business, but there's a part of his brain that is looking at the girl coming in and checking the girls. I do the same with animals.

Isabella Rossellini

I'd like this to become my principal activity: to make films about animals. Of course it's always interesting to model, but it depends who you are working with. I will continue to make acting, too, but I'm old - I'm getting tired of it.

Isabella Rossellini

When animals age, some humans see them as less valuable, less important and less entertaining.

Jenna Morasca

Animals when in company walk in a proper and sensible manner, in single file, instead of sprawling all across the road and being of no use or support to each other in case of sudden trouble or danger.

Kenneth Grahame

When I go on holiday, I go to places that have animals I'm interested in.

Dominic Monaghan

Experiments with animals have long been handicapped by our anthropocentric attitude: We often test them in ways that work fine with humans but not so well with other species.

Frans de Waal

Animals are stylized characters in a kind of old saga - stylized because even the most acute of them have little leeway as they play out their parts.

Edward Hoagland

Successive generations of middle-class parents used to foist their own favourite books on their children. But some time in the late Eighties it began to wane - not because children had lost interest in adorable animals but because most of it was available on useful, pacifying video.

Peter York

It is time my colleagues got real. All British universities doing worthwhile research use animals, and, instead of hiding, they should be boasting of their achievements.

Robert Winston

Every year, about 10 billion farm animals go through America's horrific factory farm system: cows, pigs, chickens, sheep, lamb. There, they are subjected to unimaginable and torturous confinement in vast factories where they never see the light of day. Agribusiness goes out of its way to make sure you don't see the inside of those factory farms.

Jane Velez-Mitchell

Meat production is one of the leading causes of climate change because of the destruction of the rainforest for grazing lands, the massive amounts of methane produced by farm animals and the huge amounts of water, grain and other resources required to feed animals.

Jane Velez-Mitchell

What does animal welfare have to do with food safety? The animals are the food! They are living in their own excrement, developing horrific sores, stressed out, and, therefore, more vulnerable to illness and disease.

Jane Velez-Mitchell

I couldn't watch Tom and Jerry. The cruelty was too much. I had all these strange images, of tiny animals, all mixed up.

Julie Walters

Working with children is a whole other ball game. They're like little animals. You have to keep the camera turned on them all the time. Sometimes it takes a 41-minute take to get one sentence out in a believable way.

Vera Farmiga

It is what makes us human, what distinguishes us from other animals. We can be aware of being aware.

Jon Kabat-Zinn

Animals arrived, liked the look of the place, took up their quarters, settled down, spread, and flourished. They didn't bother themselves about the past - they never do; they're too busy.

Kenneth Grahame

I started reading and learned that we don't need any of it - meat, dairy products. We get everything we need without those things - except maybe B12, but there's this whole controversy that maybe we're only getting B12 because the animals are being fed B12 supplements.

Ginnifer Goodwin

Following rules is, of course, the reason the dog is man's best friend is because the dog follows rules, and they actually do experiments on that, is that how well certain breeds of dogs follow rules, and how much they internalize them. And so many hierarchical animals, obviously they follow rules.

Frans de Waal

Most exotic animals are not particularly interested in people, which makes it hard to provoke them. Human-rearing gets them used to and sometimes imprinted on humans, which makes them potentially dangerous.

Frans de Waal

I always felt people should live with animals.

Dick Dale

I could really use a corporate sponsor. People think that because you're in the movies, you're rich. I have allocated all my resources to Shambala so the animals will always be safe.

Tippi Hedren

Never work with kids or animals.

Cat Deeley

Animals are certainly more sophisticated than we used to think. And we shouldn't lump together animals as a group. Crows and chimps and dogs are all highly intelligent in very different ways.

Alison Gopnik

I remember the evacuee children from towns and cities

throwing stones at the farm animals. When we explained that if you did that you wouldn't have any milk, meat or eggs, they soon learned to respect the animals.

Mary Wesley

I love shooting guns. Not at people or animals, but I love shooting blanks!

Maggie Q

You should always carry string, according to my archaeologist father, because then you could at least make a trap to catch animals to survive. According to my grandmother, it was clean underwear.

Ted Danson

I was blessed to grow up on a farm, and when you're a farm boy, exercise is part of your lifestyle. Like it or not, that environment makes you work out. On the farm, nature is your gym. You walk and run and swim and have to do a lot of work with animals too.

Cesar Millan

I'm not your expert on Africa or animals or whatever. I'm not a travel writer or maker of documentaries. I was someone who doesn't know very much, trying to communicate.

Michael Palin

My parents were both writers - they would type their manuscripts sitting side by side on the veranda of our house near Watford - so I wanted to do something different. I wanted to be a bluegrass singer, an architect, a landscape gardener, or to do something with animals.

Deborah Moggach

Most of what you see now emphasizes animals being dangerous to humans.

Jim Fowler

There are plenty of things you can do to help animals! The best advice that I can give right off the bat is not to get overwhelmed and feel bad when you read about all the issues.

Jenna Morasca

When you check out at PetSmart, the cashier usually asks you if you want to donate money to PetSmart charities to help save the animals. Usually, we're so busy we don't even pay attention.

Jenna Morasca

I love very much to draw animals.

Josef Albers

I have no problem with animals, I just like people more.

David Rakoff

Because animals are property, we consider as 'humane treatment' that we would regard as torture if it were inflicted on humans.

Gary L. Francione

The paparazzi is kind of crazy here in L.A., but it's nothing like it is in London. They are animals over there, it's insane.

Matthew Morrison

Traditional academic science describes human beings as highly developed animals and biological thinking machines. We appear to be Newtonian objects made of atoms, molecules, cells, tissues, and organs.

Stanislav Grof

I'm hoping one day to open my own shelter. I would be the person with the three-legged dog. I just love animals more than people; I really do.

Kaley Cuoco

I think, if you were being cruel to animals, then the thought of eating them would be horrific.

Elizabeth Hurley

I love to think that animals and humans and plants and fishes and trees and stars and the moon are all connected.

Gloria Vanderbilt

In Britain, the great hidden secret of talking animals and children's literature is how political it was in its bones, beneath the obvious cuteness.

Andrew O'Hagan

If we're not supposed to eat animals, how come they're made out of meat?

Tom Snyder

Doctors are human animals. They want to be loved, they are tribal, they instinctually favor stories over scientific evidence, they make mistakes, and even small gifts make them susceptible to being biased. If we took doctors seriously as human animals, we might hurt them - and they might hurt us - a lot less.

Alice Dreger

PETA's campaign should be included in school curricula. If we can open children's hearts and minds to animals' needs, teach them to treat a dog or a chicken as if they feel fear and love and pain - as they do - then they will grow up to understand that we are all worthy of respect.

Ingrid Newkirk

If you're going to love animals and have a life with them, the odds are you're going to lose them. It's helpful when you get a dog to accept the fact that this dog is not going to be with you your whole life.

Jon Katz

There's a long history of anthropomorphic animals in Japanese literature. The so-called 'funny animal scrolls' were the first narratives in Japanese history, and the heroes of many folk tales have animals as their companions.

Stan Sakai

Respect and affection for animals, particularly those who share our homes, recognize no geographic borders.

Nick Clooney

First and foremost I am a commercial writer, and I hope to entertain people. But having said that, I'm in love with the relationship between humans and dogs, and the more I learned about what our military working dogs are doing, I wanted to at least share with people what an important role these animals have in all our lives.

Robert Crais

Back in Australia, I did foster care for sick cats for years, and I was always most successful with the animals when I was given two - a brother and sister.

Jason Gann

I want medical experiments on animals stopped. They don't do anything, and they don't work.

Sam Simon

I remember as a little girl I could tell you the name of the dog next door, but I couldn't tell you the names of the kids. The dog was my best friend. I love animals. They give so much to you and demand so little.

Olivia Newton-John

When I was a young girl, I was so crazy about animals that I wanted to do something associated with them, and I thought of being a vet. But then again, I figured I had to go to medical school, and science wasn't a good subject for me, so I dropped the idea pretty soon and thought maybe I could be a vet's assistant.

Olivia Newton-John

There's so many issues tied to the meat industry. I mean, social, environmental, humanitarian - all of them. I know that when I'm eating that I'm not hurting the planet, I'm not hurting other people on this planet, I'm not hurting animals... and I'm not hurting nature.

Maggie Q

From my personal point of view, the Animals are dead. They killed themselves.

Eric Burdon

I really need to work. People think that I'm no longer interested in acting and only interested in working with the animals. Obviously I have given that impression, but it is not how I feel. I think I'm a good actor. I think I look OK. I don't understand why I'm not working all the time.

Tippi Hedren

I've always had a fascination for animals. I loved watching them, and even then I thought of them as beings rather than pets. I call it a birth affect!

Tippi Hedren

I do have a place in my heart for animal shelters because the job they have is impossible - so many animals that need to euthanized because don't have homes for them.

Kevin Nealon

What differentiates us from animals is the fact that we can listen to other people's dreams, fears, joys, sorrows, desires and defeats - and they in turn can listen to ours.

Henning Mankell

Humans are not the fastest or the strongest animals on the planet, but when it comes to survival, we have had the unique advantage of being clever.

David Perlmutter

I like animals, I really do, but some animals are just meant to be eaten.

Emmanuelle Vaugier

Even as a child, I felt very guilty about eating animals and never knew that there was something to do about it. And as I got older, it became clearer that there are things that I can do and choices I can make.

Mayim Bialik

I don't want any more concentration camps for animals that are cruelly treated, force-fed to fatten themselves up for our consumption.

Steve Wynn

Stars are like animals in the wild. We may see the young but never the actual birth, which is a veiled and secret event.

Heinz R. Pagels

Eventually my goal is get a place in Ojai where I can have animals and a big garden. Just drink wine all day and hang in my garden.

Michelle Branch

Humans have always used animals to depict ideas about themselves: ideas about their status, about their position in life and society and the world.

Alison Goldfrapp

Kids leave us and go off on their own lives. Family members tell us what they think of us. Animals can't do that. They really are blank canvases, and we can project anything we want onto them. So the relationship is very pure and simple.

Jon Katz

Animals play a big part in my life, on tour or at home.

Aaron Carter

My animals are a really important part of my life.

Lisa Scottoline

If you love animals, please don't eat them.

Esha Gupta

You're a good example of why some animals eat their young.

Jim Samuels

My point of view is that men are basically animals, and I'm okay with that.

Bryan Callen

Both my wife and I have a lot of compassion for animals in general.

Biz Stone

Violent predators are not like the rest of us. They kill for fun, for sport, for the sake of it. To compare them to animals is an insult to animals. To expect that we can rehabilitate them assumes a will to change.

Susan Estrich

There is a growing scientific consensus that animals have emotions and feel pain. This awareness is going to effect change: better treatment of animals in agribusiness, research and our general interaction with them. It will change the way we eat, live and preserve the planet.

April Gornik

I go on Wikipedia and alter pages of animals with fake facts that I've made up about those animals.

Kurt Braunohler

For humans and animals alike, truly vigorous, wholehearted, spontaneous play is something of a biological frill.

Robin Marantz Henig

The hardest thing about being on the road is not being with my animals.

Brandi Carlile

Stage and film are just two wildly different animals. Why compare the two?

Bebe Neuwirth

The only animals that we test on are the two of us and our kids.

Connie Sellecca

Through PETA, we rescue animals in roadside zoos and circuses. They are some of the most abused animals in the country.

Sam Simon

Besides Slayer, which is a full-time job, I raise animals. I have a ranch in Texas. My wife takes care of the animals when I'm on tour. When I get home, I become a ranch hand.

Tom Araya

It simply feels right to me to blend the glittery delights of New York City with a largely raw vegan diet - with the soul-deep conviction that animals are not ours to eat, wear, exploit or experiment on.

Victoria Moran

There's no particular evidence that any of the lower mammals or any of the other animals have any interest in aesthetics at all. But Homo sapiens does, always has and always will.

Jock Sturges

As I listened, it occurred to me that interest in and affection for the animals that share the planet with us may be a more unifying force than any other.

Nick Clooney

We cannot even predict what kinds of emergent properties would appear when animals begin interacting as part of a brain-net. In theory, you could imagine that a combination of brains could provide solutions that individual brains cannot achieve by themselves.

Miguel Nicolelis

It's one of the oldest theatrical adages: never work with children or animals.

Samantha Bond

I couldn't imagine a home without animals.

Amanda Burton

A lot of people, quite frankly, think intense attachments to animals are weird and suspect, the domain of people who can't quite handle attachments to humans.

Caroline Knapp

We do not think clearly about our moral obligations to animals.

Gary L. Francione

I did have a life before the Animals, and I'm trying constantly to prove that I have a life after the Animals. People tend to forget that I was the frontman with War for two years. People sort of have compartmental memories.

Eric Burdon

There are some songs that don't belong to The Animals that I refuse to give in to and not do. I enjoy singing other people's songs, you know. That's why they're written in the first place.

Eric Burdon

I think that now that we are seeing multimedia types of productions with videos and pictures and human beings performing the acts that animals used to perform, such as in Cirque du Soleil and other traveling troops, there is no need to parade animals around anymore in cages for personal gratification.

Montel Williams

People are beginning to realize that it's important that we see animals in a natural state - but through film, through video, through documentaries, at wildlife preserves, and through other humanely protected ways, which don't involve... performing for us.

Montel Williams

Animals interest me more than anything else.

Douglas Brinkley

I have always loved animals since I was very young.

Nafisa Joseph

When I was 8 years old, my brother was making the noises of the animals I was eating, so I decided to go vegetarian. Then I would give up because I was 8.

Alicia Silverstone

Any abuse of animals is the same as abuse of men, women, or children.

Alison Goldfrapp

Fear changes everything. We're animals, and when we get afraid we act like animals. I'm not exempt from that.

Tony Gilroy

Grissom comes from a place where we know he had a deaf mother, he was raised in a silent household, on some level, had a father who potentially was not around and he learned what he knew by himself in the back yard, with bugs and animals. He's not comfortable being a supervisor and that's his problem.

William Petersen

Shelters, conservationists, those concerned about unnecessary cruelty toward the animals we eat, and people working against species extinction fight to preserve the true riches of our planet, our real inheritance. These are big, critical goals.

April Gornik

As human pastoralists discovered 8,000 years ago, raising animals can be an efficient way of harnessing otherwise unusable resources such as grass.

Tristram Stuart

We consider all our animals to be our kids.

Eric Roberts

I love children. I'd prefer to be around children much more than adults, actually. And I like animals, too. I'm just really into beings who are at ease with themselves.

Meshell Ndegeocello

I'm always active in trying to educate people when it comes to eating animal products, testing on animals, and the health benefits of being vegan, although I'm probably not the best person to be talking about the latter at the moment.

Daniel Johns

I've always written about animals. I'm still trying to process why that is.

Tea Obreht

So for me, anything that has to do with animals, and I'm a happy camper.

Maria Menounos

The best opinion now is, that there are multitudinous forms which are not sufficiently differentiated to be distinctively either plant or animal, while, as respects ordinary plants and animals, the difficulty of laying down a definition has become far greater than ever before.

Asa Gray

Scientists who study play, in animals and humans alike, are developing a consensus view that play is something more than a way for restless kids to work off steam; more than a way for chubby kids to burn off calories; more than a frivolous luxury.

Robin Marantz Henig

I went camping in the Maasai Mara and we moved site every night. I had no idea how spectacular it would be, how removed from ordinary life, or how many animals we would see.

Georgina Chapman

There was a minor burst of macho nuttiness after 'Jaws' came out, in which people would go off in shark tournaments and come back holding the bloody heads of these animals and say, 'Look what I did.' But they've been doing that for hundreds of thousands of years anyway.

Peter Benchley

I had the best of both worlds when I was a kid. I'd spend a quiet week with my mum, then I'd go to my dad's property in the Adelaide Hills, where there were all these kids and animals running around.

Teresa Palmer

I slowly began making a few photos with animals over the years, and I liked how people reacted to them. When I would have the animals on set, I'd notice the way the models would interact with them and there was so much true emotion that you rarely see between two human beings.

Ryan McGinley

I've been out all over the world tranquilizing animals.

Jack Hanna

I spent a lot of my life - 20 years of it - in war, training army trackers and commanding a tracker unit, and then in the Game Department, tracking lions and elephants and poachers. So I've spent literally thousands of hours tracking people or animals, and training others to do it.

Allan Savory

I also love animals, and I worked at a veterinary clinic for a while, but it turns out that loving animals and removing deflated basketballs from the intestinal tracts of animals are two very different skill sets.

Karen Russell

No one would bring their horse into a studio, because they don't want to bring their prized animals into an environment where they wouldn't be comfortable or where they might panic and hurt themselves.

Jill Greenberg

In the southern half of the country perhaps no crop has larger possibilities for quick increase of production of food for both men and animals than the sweet potato.

David F. Houston

I've really become super active in rescuing animals, and it has made my life feel so much better. I can't even express to you how happy it has made me.

Carrie Ann Inaba

I am a fosterer of animals.

Bellamy Young

I think there is just a vein of humanity that really loves animals and really loves to read about them.

Sara Gruen

I'm an avid animal lover. When I was 16, I wanted to be a vet or a zookeeper. I grew up with animals. At one time we had between five and eight dogs in the house, with four cats. We're menagerie people.

Misty May-Treanor

The way animals were and are abused appalls me to this very day.

Marie Windsor

I think with 'Chunky Rice,' it felt novel to me to give this emo twist on these funny animals.

Craig Thompson

I guess growing up I realized that there is really this huge epidemic in a city like Los Angeles, and many other cities, where they put down thousands upon thousands of animals every day.

Will Estes

Most of the time, those who use animals in experiments justify that use by pointing to alleged benefits to human and animal health and the supposed necessity of using animals to obtain those benefits.

Gary L. Francione

David Gulden captures animals in all their wonder and

intrigue, without glorifying or romanticizing them. He knows Kenya's wildlife intimately, and it shows in the depth of his images. He has an artist's eye, which delivers beauty and transport in every picture.

Susan Minot

I love to cook. And I love food. I'd probably work with animals. Interior design, I'm very into that.

Gloria Votsis

There are commonalities among all the pandemics that occur, and we can learn from them. One commonality is that they all come from animals. And the other commonality is that we wait too long.

Nathan Wolfe

Towns are suffering from all these things, we should unite until we are all satisfied, man cannot be killing each other as if we were animals, as if we had no culture; that is a lack of culture.

Compay Segundo

The problem with experiments has always been that human beings make the decisions on whether or not the animals have benefitted from the treatment.

James Randi

Whether animals admit it or not, they and I communicate.

Carolyn Gold Heilbrun

The leg system of the beach animals works because of a combination of certain lengths of tubes. Because of the proportion of lengths, the animals walk smoothly. You could say that this range of numbers is their genetic code.

Theo Jansen

I think that there are many aspects to the relationship between humans and animals. But briefly, humans appear to have always been fascinated by them from the time of cave paintings and before.

Alison Goldfrapp

Animals can adapt to problems and make inventions, but often no faster than natural selection can do its work - the world acts as its own simulator in the case of natural selection.

Vernor Vinge

I invented animals and birds - I had about two dozen. After working on them for six months, I sat down and just for fun wrote two dozen poems to accompany the drawings. It was for no one to every see, but a friend sent me in to an editor.

Jack Prelutsky

The Bible tries to make humans not animals the whole time. I think it's a bit of a mistake.

Neko Case

As a kid, I loved doing puzzles, solving riddles, and reading mystery books. I also loved animals and always had pets.

Bonnie Bassler

In Kenya, where there isn't the luxury of feeding grains to animals, livestock yield more calories than they consume because they are fattened on grass and agricultural by-products inedible to humans.

Tristram Stuart

Vegetarians have been around for a very long time - Pythagoreans forbade eating animals more than 2,500 years ago - but even as the environmental evidence mounted, they didn't appear to be winning the argument.

Tristram Stuart

Viewed from a holistic ecological perspective, some meat - such as conscientiously hunted animals - involves less suffering and environmental damage than arable agriculture, while both of these are significantly less harmful than indiscriminately purchasing meat on the market.

Tristram Stuart

Sticking wires into the brain is obviously rather crude. It's hard to do in animals that run around, and there is a physical limit to the number of wires that can be inserted simultaneously.

Gero Miesenbock

I have no doubt that President George W. Bush - a man, in my experience, of extremely kind and generous instincts, and back in Austin even a rescuer of stray animals - would be appalled by the conditions of a typical American factory farm or packing plant.

Matthew Scully

For the animals, they came from the University in Uppsala and all different kinds of clinics here.

Lennart Nilsson

I personally like the idea of shellfish aquaculture. These are animals that stay quiet, they stay where you put them, and they clean up the water.

Daniel Pauly

The Weezer 'Blue' Album is a classic. I think My Morning Jacket's 'Circuital' is a great album to have. Any Led Zeppelin album. Pink Floyd 'The Dark Side Of The Moon' or 'Animals.' I always catch myself at concerts being like, 'Oh, I just stared at the drummer for 15 straight minutes.' I study them.

Christopher Mintz-Plasse

I have a great relationship with animals, and with children. I get to their level. I try to see the way a child looks at the world, it's hugely different.

Story Musgrave

Animals weren't put on this earth to entertain us.

Sheryl Lee

I grew up on a farm, so there were rifles around. Every March around springtime, there's a big hunt that goes on, and you go out and hunt down all the pheasants. I actually never shot the pheasants; I'm not a big fan of killing animals myself.

Joseph Mawle

We were in all four men with eight animals; for besides the spare horses led by Shaw and myself, an additional mule was driven along with us as a reserve in case of accident.

Francis Parkman

I'm very passionate about animals.

Emma Caulfield

Usually, I'll just sit down at a piano or with a guitar, and I'll just be relaxed and playing music. Because that's what relaxes your subconscious. That's why everyone from animals to humans love music.

Cat Power

Often extinctions in the ocean occur at the same time as those on land. Then again, the ice age extinctions lost many big animals, but not many sea faring ones.

Robert T. Bakker

People tell you not to work with children and animals, and I chose to work with a 7-year-old and several dinosaurs!

Jason O'Mara

I have agreed to lend my voice to Nature's Guard, an animated series which hopefully will go into production in the near future. The characters are all animals. My voice will be for a character named Longtail.

Jeremy Bulloch

I have always been against cruelty to animals and remain so.

Peter Baynham

I don't eat or wear animals, but I never tell people not to - that's just my view.

Loretta Swit

I was a part of that Beanie Babies generation. I had, like, 400 of them... OK, maybe not that many, but I had a lot of little stuffed animals that I liked to make talk. I was a big dork, and I still am.

Jessica Stroup

My husband says I like animals more than I like people. I take that as the compliment he means it as.

Tricia Helfer

I'm afraid of animals.

Joanna Noelle Levesque

It wasn't a problem for me drawing humans although I had originally come to the studio with the idea that what I had to offer them was my knowledge in the drawing of animals.

Marc Davis

I grew up under the British system, which I think is horrific for children - very, very strict - a system that did not recognize children as being individuals. You were small animals earning the right to be human.

Lorraine Toussaint

We moved to a place where we felt the children could have as normal an upbringing as possible. Los Angeles was not it. We live in a place with clean air and animals.

Doug Davidson

But I've worked where they've had animals before, and animal wranglers, the people who raise animals and train animals for films and television, they're all very, very professional.

M. Emmet Walsh

Whatever life may really be, it is to us an abstraction: for the word is a generalised term to signify that which is common to all animals and plants, and which is not directly operative in the inorganic world.

Oliver Joseph Lodge

Most animals are built to withstand one bad year.

John Hunter

I just think I'm better equipped to make a study of human personality than trying to get into the mind of animals.

Sara Gruen

I have met some very strange people and some very strange cats - and I'm not talking about jazz greats. I'm talking about animals that people claim have come from outer space, and boy, they're weird!

Robin Leach

I saw a bank of white light, and then I saw all my beloved animals. For a moment I stepped out of my body.

Roy Horn

Because I once became so distraught watching the film 'Watership Down,' my parents were happier to let me watch action adventures featuring humans and warriors rather than cute animals.

Rhianna Pratchett

I loved anything to do with animals from a very early age.

Edith Widder

RNA interference has proven to be a quite reliable mechanism for turning genes off in a whole variety of different plants and animals.

Craig Mello

The thing about animals is that they don't judge you. They accept you the way you are.

Wendy O. Williams

Part of my plan was not only to introduce all useful animals that I possibly could into this part of Australia, but also the most valuable plants of every description.

George Grey

I think for being not unsympathetic that their appearance may also appear, so differently it, must; similarly as with animals, which meet us in very different forms, which look somehow harmonious however all. On exactly such forms I would stand.

Ulrich Walter

Normally I play dads, good guys, and little animals.

Frank Welker

Conservatives like to think of animal protection as a trendy leftist cause, which makes it easier to brush off. And I hope that more of us will open our hearts to animals.

Matthew Scully

To the factory farmer, in contrast to the traditional farmer with his sense of honor and obligation, the animals are 'production units,' and accorded all the sympathy that term suggests.

Matthew Scully

Moreover, it thus follows that not a great deal of time was needed for the large animals of the three major parts of the world to become known to the people who spent time on the coasts of those regions.

Georges Cuvier

You can't really call yourself an environmentalist if you're still consuming animals. You just can't.

Suzy Amis

As I say, the Animals had a particular concept of themselves as a band. There was an anarchic spirit in it, which was being flattened by commercial designs, attitudes, and needs.

Alan Price

The Animals were a very separate and dissonant group at the time. We came from different backgrounds, different areas - we didn't even come from the same town, basically.

Alan Price

Fifty percent of the weight of the soybean is protein. And what a protein! No other protein that we've known comes so nearly to the basic protein of animals and humans as soybean protein.

Percy Julian

I was less successful in my attempts to effect preventive vaccination against typhus by using the virus and in trying to produce large quantities of serum using large animals.

Charles Jules Henry Nicole

With land-roaming animals, I've just read so much about the sophistication of their emotional lives and their intelligence and the way they process information that betrays a greater intelligence.

Bryan Fuller

Animals... don't have a sense of time. You just have to do things over and over with animals until they happen to do it right because they don't really know what you want.

Bruce Greenwood

I feel like, to have a career as an artist, you don't need to meet the same criteria as you do to win a singing competition. They're two very different animals.

Judith Hill

The human young must learn to perceive these affordances, in some degree at least, but the young of some animals do not have time to learn the ones that are crucial for survival.

James J. Gibson

Always wanted to be an actress or work with animals and now I get to do both.

Julia Barr

I feel blessed to have had such a background, where animals, food raising, harvesting and canning were a natural part of life.

Trina Paulus

I don't think that we really know our animals. We think we do because we're humans, and we think we can control things like that. We don't know anybody that we love. It could be a girlfriend or a cat. I think we just have to be at peace with that.

Caroline Paul

My wife and I started a program called Bears Without Borders. We raise money and hire local artisans to make stuffed animals and distribute them in their communities.

Erez Lieberman Aiden

I come from New York originally, but Californians have been wonderful about animals. These animals are so nice and so good and so sweet and intelligent. It's a crime not to help them.

Dick Van Patten

My first songs were about animals and shoes. I wrote one song about PF Flyers, and one to my fish.

Kate Micucci

There's so many mysteries related to how flies are able to make their way through the world. I'd certainly like to know a lot more about how their brain works. I'd certainly like to know a lot more about just how they're put together. I mean, these animals are basically, topologically, spheres. They don't have bones as we do, of course.

Michael Dickinson

Recording an album and doing it live are like two different animals. There are some people that are great singers live, horrible in the studio.

Frank Stallone

My mother saved hundreds of animals in her life. Wherever she encountered and injured or needy or abandoned animal, she brought it home.

Cheryl Strayed

It seems natural to surround my fictional world with animals because my reality is full of them. When I'm sitting there conceiving a story, they just pop up.

Sara Gruen

I came to join the Experience by going for an audition for Eric Burdon who was just forming the New Animals at that point, after the original Animals had broken up.

Noel Redding

I love my house. I love my family. I love my animals.

Joey King

The white man's blood and bones have begotten this bronze race, and bequeathed to it in some degree qualities, tendencies, capabilities, such as are the inheritance of the highest order of human animals.

Fanny Kemble

In a few generations more, there will probably be no room at all allowed for animals on the earth: no need of them, no toleration of them.

Marie Louise

We eat animals because they taste good. And if that's O.K., what's wrong with wearing fur? We need as a society to think seriously about our institutionalized animal use.

Gary L. Francione

Ever occur to you why some of us can be this much concerned with animals suffering? Because government is not. Why not? Animals don't vote.

Will Harvey

Kip Keino, Moses Tanui, Paul Tergat, they all come from my tribe. Some say it is the food we eat that makes us strong, the way we live. In the history of our people we wear no clothes and we are used to drinking the blood of animals.

Martin Lel

If you're a wildlife filmmaker and you're going out into the field to film animals, especially behavior, it helps to have a fundamental background on who these animals are, how they work and, you know, a bit about their behaviors.

Mike deGruy

If you're going to make a lot of films about a particular group of animals, you might as well pick one that's fairly common. And octopus are: they live in all the oceans. They also live deep. And I can't say octopus are responsible for my really strong interest in getting in subs and going deep, but whatever the case, I like that.

Mike deGruy

If I wasn't acting, I'd try and be a footballer. I wouldn't be a musician because I can't write my own music. Realistically, I'd probably do something with dogs, like a vet or something. I love animals.

Jamie Blackley

The things that are really important to me are my man, my animals and my books. I don't need anything else.

Mary Crosby

I just don't think animals should be slaughtered for their fur.

Dominique Swain

I am deathly allergic to cats. I mean, I love all animals, but they're not my animal of choice.

Rick Hoffman

Animals are the best actors. They never lie, they're always present, and they listen. That's a lot more than a lot of actors can say for themselves.

Graham Phillips

From an egotistical point of view, I'm always interested in roles that push me as a person. I'm interested in humans as animals and as products of society.

Tom Cullen

Peter's fear of the animals which were shown him was probably not a directly conditioned fear.

Mary C. Jones

I never do the cute thing with animals; they are interesting shapes. I just use their profile. Because German shepherds are so easily recognizable, they would fall outside my purview.

Billy Al Bengston

I do remember how it was to be poor. I do remember that in

my early years, we had to grow and raise all of our food, even our animals. And I remember in my early life, we didn't even have electricity. So it was very, very hard times then.

Dolly Parton

There are some four million different kinds of animals and plants in the world. Four million different solutions to the problems of staying alive.

David Attenborough

With the demise of the biblical religions that have provided the American people with their core values since their country's inception, we are reverting to the pagan worldview. Trees and animals are venerated, while man is simply one more animal in the ecosystem - and largely a hindrance, not an asset.

Dennis Prager

Yes, I've kissed a lot of guys. I like to kiss, but that's it. I don't go home with anyone. I sleep with my animals, like my baby monkey, Brigitte Bardot.

Paris Hilton

I used to think I was ugly. I thought I looked like a camel. A person who doesn't love themselves, they will see anything that pops up on their face. I've seen squirrels, I've seen a bird, and I've seen all kinds of animals on my face. But that is the result of self-hate. I've learned to say: 'You know what? I am a beautiful black woman'.

Mary J. Blige

The musician is perhaps the most modest of animals, but he is also the proudest. It is he who invented the sublime art of ruining poetry.

Erik Satie

I've loved singing since forever. Whether it was with my sisters while cleaning the kitchen, putting shows on for my stuffed animals, writing songs about my stuffed animals, starting an a capella group with my cousins while on vacation, or awkwardly singing along to karaoke tracks alone in my bedroom - singing always found a way into my life.

Kina Grannis

The dog has got more fun out of Man than Man has got out

of the dog, for the clearly demonstrable reason that Man is the more laughable of the two animals.

James Thurber

Dogs and other animals - goats, donkeys, cows, a grumpy rooster - continue to change my writing life.

Jon Katz

You cannot share your life with a dog, as I had done in Bournemouth, or a cat, and not know perfectly well that animals have personalities and minds and feelings.

Jane Goodall

Animals are sentient, intelligent, perceptive, funny and entertaining. We owe them a duty of care as we do to children.

Michael Morpurgo

It is much easier to show compassion to animals. They are never wicked.

Haile Selassie

Studying cows, pigs and chickens can help an actor develop his character. There are a lot of things I learned from animals. One was that they couldn't hiss or boo me.

James Dean

Let's get into talking about how autism is similar animal behavior. The thing is I don't think in a language, and animals don't think in a language. It's sensory based thinking, thinking in pictures, thinking in smells, thinking in touches. It's putting these sensory based memories into categories.

Temple Grandin

I always wanted to be a zookeeper when I was growing up, and I've wound up a zookeeper! I've been working with the Los Angeles Zoo for 45 years! I'm the luckiest old broad on two feet because my life is divided absolutely in half - half animals and half show business. You can't ask for better than two things you love the most.

Betty White

Wild animals never kill for sport. Man is the only one to whom the torture and death of his fellow creatures is amusing in itself.

James Anthony Froude

We must plant the sea and herd its animals using the sea as farmers instead of hunters. That is what civilization is all about - farming replacing hunting.

Jacques Yves Cousteau

I really love animals. My cat is my little soul mate. He's not just a cat, he's my friend.

Tracey Emin

I'm always pushing for human responsibility. Given that chimpanzees and many other animals are sentient and sapient, then we should treat them with respect.

Jane Goodall

We're losing biodiversity globally at an alarming rate, and we need a cornucopia of different plants and animals, for the planet's health and our own.

Diane Ackerman

Goats are the cable talk show panelists of the animal world, ready at a moment's notice to interject, interrupt, and opine. They have something to say about everything, little of it complimentary. They are the most impertinent animals I have ever known.

Jon Katz

When you're writing a book, with people in it as opposed to animals, it is no good having people who are ordinary, because they are not going to interest your readers at all. Every writer in the world has to use the characters that have something interesting about them, and this is even more true in children's books.

Roald Dahl

I have found that, in the composition of the human body as compared with the bodies of animals, the organs of sense are duller and coarser. Thus, it is composed of less ingenious instruments, and of spaces less capacious for receiving the faculties of sense.

Leonardo da Vinci

I gave my beauty and my youth to men. I am going to give

my wisdom and experience to animals.

Brigitte Bardot

I don't care how hot a girl is - if she doesn't like animals, it would be a major, major problem.

Ian Somerhalder

I'm definitely going for shots that I haven't seen before, but they're animals. I have no control over what they give me and what they do for me, which is great. Whereas, when I shoot people, I control the situation for the most part - from telling them where to stand to where to look. For the animals, they're dictating me. I have to adapt to them.

Michael Muller

Working with animals forces an actor to work harder because you have to be quick when it comes to improvisation, and you can't break character - at all.

Kyle Massey

Birds are hard to draw. I read recently that Katsuhiro Otomo also says he has trouble drawing animals, and while it made me feel better, it didn't make it easier for me.

Stuart Immonen

There are many things I love in this world. Music, acting, and animals are at the top of that list.

Orlando Brown

The tabloids are like animals, with their own behavioural patterns. There's no point in complaining about them, any more than complaining that lions might eat you.

David Mellor

How much will you give for the lives of your childrens children, which is yourself? How much are people willing to give up for air, earth, water, animals, and the coming generations? I think the answer to that is pretty clear.

Lynette Fromme

The desire to take medicine is perhaps the greatest feature which distinguishes man from animals.

William Osler

My music is best understood by children and animals.

Igor Stravinsky

I'm a vegetarian and very much active in regards to how I feel about animal rights and protecting animals and giving animals a voice. But at the same time, I appreciate and respect other people's decisions to eat meat. The only thing that I hope is that people are educated, that they're aware, that they're living a conscious lifestyle.

Abbie Cornish

Man's unique reward, however, is that while animals survive by adjusting themselves to their background, man survives by adjusting his background to himself.

Ayn Rand

Obstacles are like wild animals. They are cowards but they will bluff you if they can. If they see you are afraid of them... they are liable to spring upon you; but if you look them squarely in the eye, they will slink out of sight.

Orison Swett Marden

I love all animals. I have a fascination with fish, birds, whales - sentient life - insects, reptiles.

Nicolas Cage

When we see animals doing remarkable things, how do we know if we're simply seeing tricks or signs of real intelligence? Are talented animals just obeying commands, or do they have some kind of deeper understanding? One of the biggest challenges for animal researchers is to come up with tests that can distinguish between the two.

Neil deGrasse Tyson

Puerto Ricans who find they can no longer afford to keep their pets often choose to drop their dogs, sometimes even whole litters of puppies, at a beach - sometimes under cover of night, in secret - rather than surrender the animal to a city or state-run shelter where the animals will face grim conditions and almost certain death by euthanasia.

Juliana Hatfield

No, I'm not very productive at all. I'm probably like an animal. I mean, great animals in the ocean feed all the time. I'm someone who procrastinates, worries, for most of a month, and then I'll have a flurry of manic productivity with a sense of great urgency and fear for, like, two days.

Jonathan Ames

Those who wish to pet and baby wild animals 'love' them. But those who respect their natures and wish to let them live normal lives, love them more.

Edwin Way Teale

Human beings are the only animals of which I am thoroughly and cravenly afraid.

George Bernard Shaw

I am not a vegetarian because I love animals; I am a vegetarian because I hate plants.

A. Whitney Brown

I hate having to do small talk. I'd rather talk about deep subjects. I'd rather talk about meditation, or the world, or the trees or animals, than small, inane, you know, banter.

Ellen DeGeneres

We're so much more likely to feel sympathy for an animal than another person; thus, the best fiction uses animals to define truly humane behavior.

Chuck Palahniuk

The best thing about animals is that they don't talk much.

Thornton Wilder

Animals that we eat are raised for food in the most economical way possible, and the serious food producers do it in the most humane way possible. I think anyone who is a carnivore needs to understand that meat does not originally come in these neat little packages.

Julia Child

All our knowledge merely helps us to die a more painful death than animals that know nothing.

Maurice Maeterlinck

The difference between humans and wild animals is that humans pray before they commit murder.

Friedrich Durrenmatt

I wasn't always a vegetarian. I didn't care about animals one way or the other; they were part of the scenery, until one day on tour, I saw a baby panda. I thought that it was the most fabulous animal in the world and made a different kind of connection. I began to understand how animals were part of the greater scheme, and I stopped eating them.

Grace Slick

A plague on eminence! I hardly dare cross the street anymore without a convoy, and I am stared at wherever I go like an idiot member of a royal family or an animal in a zoo; and zoo animals have been known to die from stares.

Igor Stravinsky

People always joke that 'dog' spells 'god' backwards. They should consider that it might be the higher power coming down to see just how well they do, what kind of people they are. The animals are right here, right in front of us. And how we treat these companions is a test.

Linda Blair

Animals are in possession of themselves; their soul is in possession of their body. But they have no right to their life, because they do not will it.

Georg Wilhelm Friedrich Hegel

Most Africans don't get to see these wild animals at all. Once they see and learn about them, they are much more likely to become involved in protecting the environment.

Jane Goodall

I do love one-upmanship sometimes, like when you see kids breakdancing and who can do the best tricks. It's common, it's in our nature as animals, like the birds of paradise who've got the best feathers and that sort of stuff. But it's fun when it's impulsive and it's about fun.

Bjork

I love goats, something I did not do for the great bulk of my years on this planet. I love their insouciance, their curiosity, their authority issues, their rapt fascination with almost everything. Living with all of these other animals who revere me for taking care of them, it's refreshing to have goats who regularly nip the hand that feeds them.

Jon Katz

Millions of animals are euthanized every year because shelters can't find homes for them. Buying animals from pet stores also tends to support puppy and cat mills, many of which have deplorable conditions for animals, which shouldn't be tolerated.

Laura Mennell

Americans! They want to go 600 miles an hour, and they don't know how to walk! Look at them in the street. Bent over. Coughing! Young men with gray faces! Why can't they look at the animals? Look at a cat. Look at any animal. The only animal that doesn't hold its stomach in is the pig.

Joseph Pilates

Animals are my friends... and I don't eat my friends.

George Bernard Shaw

When man learns to understand and control his own behavior as well as he is learning to understand and control the behavior of crop plants and domestic animals, he may be justified in believing that he has become civilized.

Ayn Rand

The animals of the world exist for their own reasons. They were not made for humans any more than black people were made for white, or women created for men.

Alice Walker

The fate of animals is of greater importance to me than the fear of appearing ridiculous; it is indissolubly connected with the fate of men.

Emile Zola

Research has shown that a barren environment is much more damaging to baby animals than it is to adult animals. It does not hurt the adult animals the same way it damages babies.

Temple Grandin

Teach your children how to behave with animals. Adopt a pet. Don't go buy one. Please. That's a sin. Let's get these puppy mills out of business.

Shelley Morrison

Researching 'Lone Wolf,' I was amazed at how thoughtful and intelligent these animals are. There has never been a documented attack against a human by a wolf that wasn't provoked by the human.

Jodi Picoult

Wild animals would not stay in a country where there were so many people. Pa did not like to stay, either. He liked a country where the wild animals lived without being afraid.

Laura Ingalls Wilder

Endurance, after all, is the only reason we even exist. We think of ourselves as nature's deadliest animals, but the truth is, a naked human is the biggest wimp in the wild. We have no fangs, no claws, no strength, and no speed.

Christopher McDougall

Animal abuse is rampant in the U.S., right under everyone's eyes, for the entertainment of the public. The brutal confinement and pain of training methods of wild animals in the circus, the aquatic and theatrical shows, leads to retaliation by the animals. Eventually they find the right time to strike out, and they will.

Tippi Hedren

I blame it on Walt Disney, where animals are given human qualities. People don't understand that a wild animal is not something that is nice to pat. It can seriously harm you.

James Cameron

Just about every children's book in my local bookstore has an animal for its hero. But then, only a few feet away in the cookbook section, just about every cookbook includes recipes for cooking animals. Is there a more illuminating illustration of our paradoxical relationship with the nonhuman world?

Jonathan Safran Foer

Psychology is the science of the intellects, characters and behavior of animals including man.

Edward Thorndike

Animals have genes for altruism, and those genes have been selected in the evolution of many creatures because of the advantage they confer for the continuing survival of the species.

Lewis Thomas

Unfortunately, I'm allergic to all animals and even some people.

Wentworth Miller

I have always been an animal lover. I had a hard time disassociating the animals I cuddled with - dogs and cats, for example - from the animals on my plate, and I never really cared for the taste of meat. I always loved my Brussels sprouts.

Kristen Bell

I try to only eat animals that are vegan. I'm probably the opposite of a vegan.

Jim Gaffigan

People don't know about the human part of me that really cares about the world. For instance, I don't know what I feel about wearing my furs anymore. I worked so hard to have a fur coat, and I don't want to wear it anymore because I'm so wrapped up in the animals. I have real deep thoughts about it because I care about the world and nature.

Diana Ross

In my life outdoors, I've observed that animals of almost any variety will stand in a windy place rather than in a protected, windless area infested with biting insects. They would rather be annoyed by the wind than bitten.

Tim Cahill

I see a lot of damage to Mother Earth. I see water being taken from creeks where water belongs to animals, not to oil companies.

Winona LaDuke

Nature makes only dumb animals. We owe the fools to society.

Honore de Balzac

Man is an exception, whatever else he is. If he is not the image of God, then he is a disease of the dust. If it is not true that a divine being fell, then we can only say that one of the animals went entirely off its head.

Gilbert K. Chesterton

Often and often afterwards, the beloved Aunt would ask me why I had never told anyone how I was being treated. Children tell little more than animals, for what comes to them they accept as eternally established.

Rudyard Kipling

Because I wanted to have a place that I could create everything that I that I never had as a child. So, you see rides. You see animals. There's a movie theater.

Michael Jackson

It is inexcusable for scientists to torture animals; let them make their experiments on journalists and politicians.

Henrik Ibsen

Men are rather reasoning than reasonable animals, for the most part governed by the impulse of passion.

Alexander Hamilton

Chinese civilisation is so systematic that wild animals have been abolished on principle.

Aleister Crowley

The animals that depend on instinct have an inherent knowledge of the laws of economics and of how to apply them; Man, with his powers of reason, has reduced economics to the level of a farce which is at once funnier and more tragic than Tobacco Road.

James Thurber

Having travelled to some 20 African countries, I find myself, like so many other visitors to Africa before me, intoxicated with the continent. And I am not referring to the animals, as much as I have been enthralled by them during safaris in Kenya, Tanzania and Zimbabwe. Rather, I am referring to the African peoples.

Dennis Prager

People who care about animals tend to care about people. They don't care about animals to the exclusion of people. Caring is not a finite resource and, even more than that, it's like a muscle: the more you exercise it, the stronger it gets.

Jonathan Safran Foer

All the arguments to prove man's superiority cannot shatter this hard fact: in suffering the animals are our equals.

Peter Singer

Books have the same enemies as people: fire, humidity, animals, weather, and their own content.

Paul Valery

I am just like my mother. She raised me to love and take care of animals, especially the ones that need it the most and so I started Eddie's Rescue Ranch. We take in animals that need extra care and attention and the animals that get left behind.

Kelly Clarkson

I don't believe in pets. I like animals to be wild and free.

John Lydon

To err is human also in so far as animals seldom or never err, or at least only the cleverest of them do so.

Georg C. Lichtenberg

If you call a cat, he may not come. Which doesn't happen

with dogs. They're different types of animals. Cats are very sexy I think too in the way they move.

Antonio Banderas

The only animals I'm not comfortable with are parrots, but I'm learning as I go. I'm getting better and better at 'em. I really am.

Steve Irwin

I was brought up to understand Darwin's theory of evolution. I spent hours and hours in the Natural History Museum in London looking at the descriptions of how different kinds of animals had evolved, looking at the sequence of fossil bones looking gradually more and more and more and more like the modern fossil.

Jane Goodall

Art owes its origin to Nature herself... this beautiful creation, the world, supplied the first model, while the original teacher was that divine intelligence which has not only made us superior to the other animals, but like God Himself, if I may venture to say it.

Giorgio Vasari

Cows are gentle, interesting animals.

Ingrid Newkirk

Nevertheless most of the evergreen forests of the north must always remain the home of wild animals and trappers, a backward region in which it is easy for a great fur company to maintain a practical monopoly.

Ellsworth Huntington

We're the only species who follow unstable leaders. This is true - it has little to do with America - around the world, pack leaders are unstable. Animals don't follow that.

Cesar Millan

Pigs prefer to wallow in clean mud, but if nothing else is available, they will frequently wallow in their own urine, giving rise to the notion that they are dirty animals.

Marvin Harris

You know, having raised animals all my life for 50-something years, I would say that you know, I'm fascinated by cats.

Jack Hanna

I probably shouldn't say this about all animals, but at least the farm animals that I've hung out with, and even when I go to the zoo usually, they're like a blank slate. I guess that's why I like them. They're puppets, and you can imagine them being anything you want.

Kristen Schaal

According to the 'food waste pyramid,' ensuring that food is eaten by people is the top priority. Failing that, the next best thing is to feed it to farm animals.

Tristram Stuart

Only the most acute and active animals are capable of boredom. - A theme for a great poet would be God's boredom on the seventh day of creation.

Lewis Cass

Animals of all classes, old and young, shrink with instinctive fear from any strange object approaching them.

William Henry Hudson

While we ourselves are the living graves of murdered animals, how can we expect any ideal living conditions on this earth?

George Bernard Shaw

We are not animals. We are not a product of what has happened to us in our past. We have the power of choice.

Stephen Covey

Anyone who hates children and animals can't be all bad.

W. C. Fields

A man is ethical only when life, as such, is sacred to him, that of plants and animals as that of his fellow men, and when he devotes himself helpfully to all life that is in need of help.

Albert Schweitzer

The theoretical understanding of the world, which is the

aim of philosophy, is not a matter of great practical importance to animals, or to savages, or even to most civilised men.

Bertrand Russell

Men feel that cruelty to the poor is a kind of cruelty to animals. They never feel that it is an injustice to equals; nay it is treachery to comrades.

Gilbert K. Chesterton

Humans are the only animals that have children on purpose with the exception of guppies, who like to eat theirs.

P. J. O'Rourke

Just as our ancient ancestors drew animals on cave walls and carved animals from wood and bone, we decorate our homes with animal prints and motifs, give our children stuffed animals to clutch, cartoon animals to watch, animal stories to read.

Diane Ackerman

It's perfectly obvious that there is some genetic factor that distinguishes humans from other animals and that it is language-specific. The theory of that genetic component, whatever it turns out to be, is what is called universal grammar.

Noam Chomsky

We lavish on animals the love we are afraid to show to people. They might not return it; or worse, they might.

Mignon McLaughlin

Ever occur to you why some of us can be this much concerned with animals suffering? Because government is not. Why not? Animals don't vote.

Paul Harvey

People love their animals so much so that they put little clothes on them and necklaces and booties and things like that. And if you love your animal, then you should feed them something that's not dangerous for them. There's a lot of poisonous stuff that they're putting in a lot of that food, those by-products.

Ellen DeGeneres

If we're destroying our trees and destroying our environment and hurting animals and hurting one another and all that stuff, there's got to be a very powerful energy to fight that. I think we need more love in the world.

Ellen DeGeneres

People often say that humans have always eaten animals, as if this is a justification for continuing the practice. According to this logic, we should not try to prevent people from murdering other people, since this has also been done since the earliest of times.

Isaac Bashevis Singer

God looks after children, animals and idiots.

Lou Holtz

Animals, in their generation, are wiser than the sons of men; but their wisdom is confined to a few particulars, and lies in a very narrow compass.

Joseph Addison

Animals have never betrayed me. They are an easy prey, as

I have been throughout my career. So we feel the same. I love them.

Brigitte Bardot

We are a unique ape. We have language. Other animals have systems of communication that fall far short of that. They don't have the same ability to communicate complicated conditionals and what-ifs and talk about things that are not present.

Richard Dawkins

The person who thinks I worship the devil and kill animals is just as important as someone who makes an interpretation that's closer to what I intended.

Marilyn Manson

I hope to make people realize how totally helpless animals are, how dependent on us, trusting as a child must that we will be kind and take care of their needs.

James Herriot

The only honest reaction and true loyalty we get is from

our animals. Once they're your friends, you can do no wrong.

Dick Van Patten

If I could stomach the awful part of being a veterinarian, which involves sticking your hand up animals' behinds, I would be a vet.

Allison Janney

Zoos are becoming facsimiles - or perhaps caricatures - of how animals once were in their natural habitat. If the right policies toward nature were pursued, we would need no zoos at all.

Michael J. Fox

Mankind's true moral test, its fundamental test (which lies deeply buried from view), consists of its attitude towards those who are at its mercy: animals. And in this respect mankind has suffered a fundamental debacle, a debacle so fundamental that all others stem from it.

Milan Kundera

Humans aren't as good as we should be in our capacity to empathize with feelings and thoughts of others, be they humans or other animals on Earth.

Neil deGrasse Tyson

When I see professional clowns, mimes, or people who makes ballon animals, I think of their relatives and how disappointed they must be.

Jimmy Fallon

I could do terrible things to people who dump unwanted animals by the roadside.

James Herriot

I've always thought a hotel ought to offer optional small animals. I mean a cat to sleep on your bed at night, or a dog of some kind to act pleased when you come in. You ever notice how a hotel room feels so lifeless?

Anne Tyler

I remember that. I was talking to him and I said how great it would be if actors had a tail because I have animals and a tail is so expressive. On a cat you can tell everything. You can tell if they're annoyed. You can tell whether they're scared.

Christopher Walken

The countenances of children, like those of animals, are masks, not faces, for they have not yet developed a significant profile of their own.

W. H. Auden

When you get into the whole field of exploring, probably 90 percent of the kinds of organisms, plants, animals and especially microorganisms and tiny invertebrate animals are unknown. Then you realize that we live on a relatively unexplored plan.

E. O. Wilson

We have abolished the death penalty for humans, so why should it continue for animals?

Brigitte Bardot

I urge you to ask yourself just how honorable it is to

preside over the abuse and suffering of animals.

Richard Pryor

Brute animals have the vowel sounds; man only can utter consonants.

Samuel Taylor Coleridge

Animals outline their territories with their excretions, humans outline their territories by ink excretions on paper.

Robert Anton Wilson

Once I showed up at my sister's with a baby rabbit I had bought from some children because its ears were cold. I put the rabbit on a hot water bottle and massaged its ears for quite a while. After all, I knew that all healthy animals had warm ears.

Juliette Gordon Low

China once again disgusts the world, portraying the image of a cruel, perverted people devoid of any feelings towards animals.

Brigitte Bardot

If you love animals, obviously it doesn't make sense to hurt them.

Steven Patrick Morrissey

I love animals, but I don't really like riding animals. Like, I don't love being on a horse - it's just not my thing.

Miley Cyrus

The belief that the animals exist because God created them - and that he created them so we can better meet our needs - is contrary to our scientific understanding of evolution and, of course, to the fossil record, which shows the existence of non-human primates and other animals millions of years before there were any human beings at all.

Peter Singer

I love sports. I love animals. I love kids. I want to save the world. So how do I combine all those things? I don't know.

Joan Jett

I'm not an animal lover if that means you think things are

nice if you can pat them, but I am intoxicated by animals.

David Attenborough

I've seen people that don't treat their animals well and yet their animals are still just as loving to them even though they're not treated that well. It's very hard to find that kind of loyalty and love and affection in human beings.

Dick Van Patten

I only want to protect animals from barbarous, cruel, inhuman and backward rituals.

Brigitte Bardot

I hope to bring much more attention to important issues and change for issues and practices that are harming animals.

Kesha

I don't wear fur and I understand their cause. I am the biggest animal lover in the world. I have four dogs and two horses, and I have rescued animals all my life.

Gisele Bundchen

Religions in general have to rediscover their roots. In Hinduism and the Koran, animals are described as equals. If you walk into a cathedral and look at the decorations of early Christianity, there are vines, animals, creatures and birds thriving all over the stonework.

Margaret Atwood

First I wanted to be a veterinarian. And then I realized you had to give them shots to put them to sleep, so I decided I'd just buy a bunch of animals and have them in my house instead.

Paris Hilton

Confining marine animals to tanks and separating them from their families and their natural surroundings, just so people can watch them swim in endless circles, teaches us far more about humans than it does about animals - and the lesson is not a flattering one.

Pamela Anderson

Animals do not admire each other. A horse does not admire its companion.

Thomas Mann